# PILGRIMS IN THE HOLY LAND

## Bernard Jackson

GEOFFREY
CHAPMAN

*To my three sons:*
*Thomas, William and Oliver*

*Geoffrey Chapman*
An imprint of Cassell Publishers Limited
Villiers House, 41–47 Strand, London WC2N 5JE, England

© Bernard Jackson 1991

All rights reserved. No part of this publication may be reproduced or transmitted in any form or by any means, electronic or mechanical including photocopying, recording or any information storage or retrieval system, without prior permission in writing from the publishers.

First published 1991

*British Library Cataloguing in Publication Data*
Jackson, Bernard *1940–*
 Pilgrim in the Holy Land.
 1. Palestine. Description & travel
  I. Title
  915.6940454

ISBN 0–225–66605–7

Typeset by Fakenham Photosetting Limited, Fakenham, Norfolk
Printed and bound in Great Britain by
Biddles Ltd, Guildford and King's Lynn

# Contents

**Foreword** v

**Acknowledgements** ix

**Introduction**  A different kind of holiday  1

**DAY 1**  Jerusalem and Bethlehem  7

**DAY 2**  Bethany, Jericho, Masada and the Dead Sea  20

**DAY 3**  Dominus Flevit, Gethsemane and the real Way of the Cross  33

**DAY 4**  A meeting point of languages and faiths  56

**DAY 5**  Emmaus, Caesarea and Galilee  75

**DAY 6**  Capernaum  86

**DAY 7**  Nazareth and Mount Tabor  96

**DAY 8**  The Crusaders and Mount Carmel  105

**DAY 9**  Caesarea Philippi and fish beside the lake  114

### MAPS

The Holy Land  iv

Jerusalem and the Via Dolorosa  x

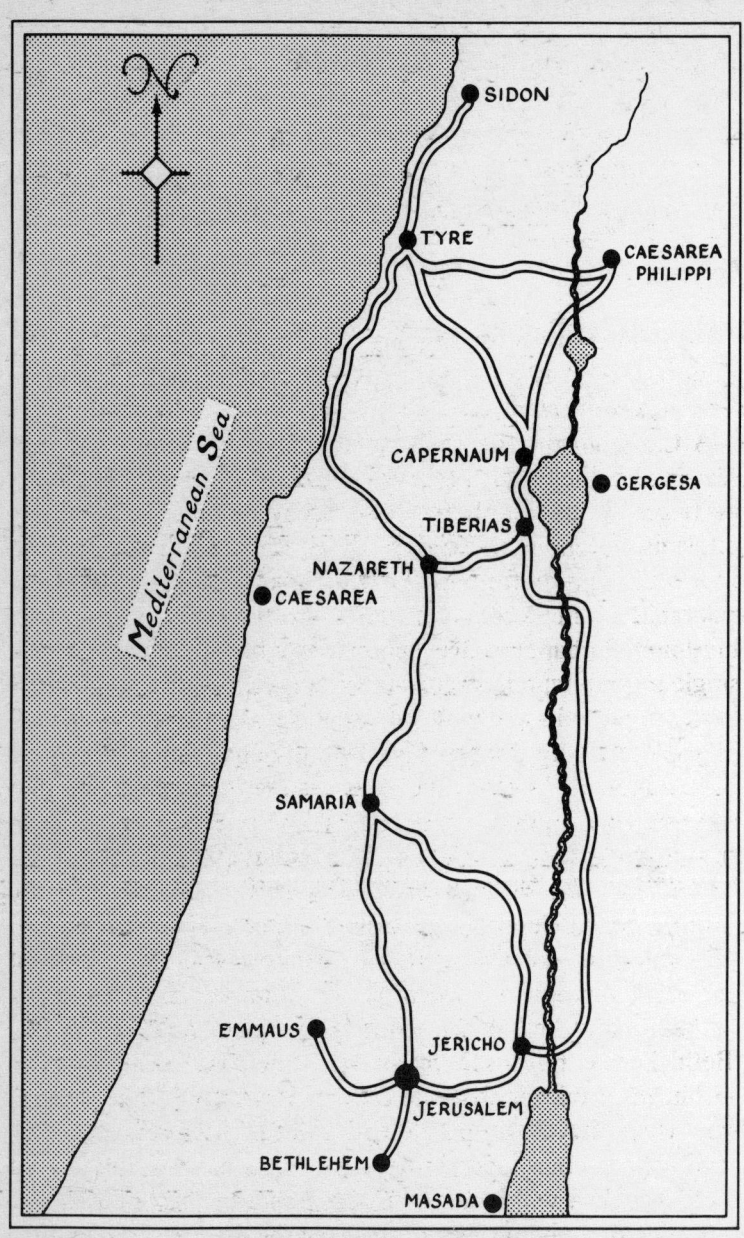

THE HOLY LAND

# Foreword

*'... giving him [Jesus] to be born in Bethlehem for our salvation, in Jerusalem to die upon the cross and to rise again for all the human race ...'*

Those words come from the Thanksgiving prayer in the Eucharist as it is celebrated in the Anglican cathedral of St George's, Jerusalem.

A Christian pilgrim to Palestine may have many different reasons for their visit. After many years of leading such pilgrimages, I suspect there are as many motives as there are pilgrims. Even in these days of jet air travel, comfortable hotels and air-conditioned coaches many people make considerable sacrifices to go on what is for them 'the journey of a lifetime'. Perhaps I have been lucky, but I cannot recall a single pilgrim who has returned either wishing they had never been or regarding the whole exercise as misguided. Every pilgrim, to some degree, finds it a life-changing experience. 'Life will never be the same again' is a sentiment that is often expressed by a pilgrim returning home after ten or fourteen days in Jerusalem and Galilee. Why should this be so?

A major part of the answer lies in the words from the 'Liturgy for St George's, Jerusalem' quoted above. When you visit Palestine you are directly confronted with the drama of our salvation. As you worship, for example, in St George's Cathedral and hear those words you cannot help but think: 'Bethlehem is but a few miles down the road and Calvary is within easy walking distance here in Jerusalem'. The same is true wherever you go in Palestine. All the places that we have known from childhood through the pages of the Bible are all there—packed within a land that is about the size of Wales! I can think of no better way of 'making the liturgy come to life'. When a pilgrim returns from Palestine and goes to church hardly a service will go by without thinking: 'I remember Jericho, Capernaum, Caesarea Philippi . . . etc.'.

So one very straightforward reason for pilgrimage is hat pilgrims gain a greater understanding of the Bible by visiting the place 'where it all happened'. Jerome, himself a resident of Bethlehem in the fourth century AD, wrote: 'One understands holy scripture better when one has seen with one's own eyes Judaea and contemplated the ruins of ancient cities'. It needs an expert guide with good communication skills to stand in front of an excavation trench and make it come alive. A pilgrim blessed by having such a guide will have his or her prayer 'to make the Book live' answered in ways that would be impossible through referring to even the most accurate Bible dictionary.

But there is more to pilgrimage than that. Christians do not worship a book! The essence of pilgrimage is that it is an activity that helps one to reach out towards God and to deepen one's relationship with him. That cannot be forced. A pilgrim to Palestine will find that the places one visits speak for themselves. Granted that you need a sympathetic and knowledgeable leader who can impart just enough information to allow this happen. But 'letting a site speak for itself' and make its own impact is the aim of every spiritual leader. Over many years I have wrestled with the problem of what to do at holy places in terms of spiritual exercise. This has resulted in a book of my own entitled *Praying at the Holy Places* which is due to be published soon. Bible reading, meditation and silence are some of the essential ingredients—but not always easy to achieve in a hubbub of tourists!

So far I have used the term 'Palestine' and not 'Israel' or 'Holy Land'. Although 'Holy Land' trips most easily off the tongue, it is all too easy to sentimentalize the term and forget that one is visiting a modern state (Israel) with another 'state within a state' (Palestine). To my mind it is little less than an outrage to treat a visit to the Holy Land solely as a means of personal spiritual experience and yet ignore the almost insoluble problems within this tiny Middle Eastern country. A vital ingredient to any pilgrimage today is to pray for the peace of Jerusalem intelligently and compassionately.

In the Old Testament we have the picture of an 'eternal triangle': God—land—People. A key idea is that of *eretz Israel* (land of Israel). The land is God-given, it is the promised land. The faith is linked to the land. But the Christian has no 'holy land'—every place is holy. A paradox remains, however, and it is one that has been called 'the sacrament of geography'. The key here is the mystery of the incarnation. God became man in a particular place at a particular time in history. The point of pilgrimage is to recover the significance of Jesus as the Christ.

It is not always easy to do this at 'holy places'. Some of the places seem anything but holy. Sometimes there is more than one place for the same event. At some of them our credulity will be stretched; at others we shall be on much firmer historical ground. At all of them we must discover the holy thing behind the holy place.

What matters more than holy places is holy people. You will meet some of them in this book—Christian, Muslim and Jew. They are the 'living stones' who are infinitely more important than any ancient ruin. A pilgrimage which concentrates on ancient ruins (fascinating though they are) at the expense of people of faith will be in danger of missing the point. In a booklet that is sent to many Holy Land pilgrims before they set out the words of an anonymous Galilean believer are quoted: 'People normally come for holy shrines and holy places. For us local Christians these are just sand and stone that are meaningless without a Christian community which witnesses to the presence of the Lord here today.' There is a grave danger today that holy places will become museums unless there are local people to maintain a living tradition of worship. The aim of one company today that promotes Christian pilgrimage is 'communication through travel'. Pilgrimage for most of us is a communal and not a solitary exercise. To meet other pilgrims within a group is inevitable. We should also go out of our way to meet local Christians, the 'living stones' who are always keen to share their faith and their concerns with us.

As Christians we must never forget to pray for the peace of this land. We are faced with a tragic situation, and the fact of tragedy is the ultimate significance of Gethsemane, one of the 'holy places' every pilgrim visits. What are we to do with tragedy? Justice is impossible without injustice—on both sides. Our Christian vocation is to be reconcilers—to seek reconciliation. Our pilgrimage should not only draw us nearer to God but also nearer to our 'neighbour'.

It was a salutary experience for me to lead this particular pilgrimage. I was asked to do so at just a couple of weeks' notice because the appointed leader could not go. At the same time I was told 'You will have to cope with a radio chappie who is doing a documentary on pilgrimage'. What that really meant was that everywhere we went I was liable to find a microphone thrust under my nose and had the feeling that everything I said was being taken down to be used in evidence . . .! It is the skill of a broadcaster to make one feel that the microphone simply isn't there. Bernard Jackson achieved that aim with consummate skill. I wholeheartedly recommend his book as giving you an insight into what pilgrimage today is all about. It is not a guidebook—there are more than enough of them about already. Rather it is a timely book of experiencing what being a 'Pilgrim in the Holy Land' today is all about. Many potential pilgrims today have second thoughts about making a pilgrimage to a troubled land. If this book convinces you that such a visit is [in normal circumstances] not only possible but safe—and can even be fun—then it will have achieved one of its aims. If it helps you to 'pray for the peace of Jerusalem' more intelligently than before, even better. And if you are simply looking for 'a good read', I can guarantee that you will find that too!

The land that is the theme of this book is constantly in the news. Expert after expert have their say. Even I have been labelled an 'expert' and consulted about all manner of things concerning the Holy Land. It is often far more helpful to forget the experts for a while and read the words of an eyewitness whose objective is 'to tell it as it is'. This is a 'cameo' of what it was like to be a pilgrim to Palestine at a particular time, with a particular group and with a particular leader. Such accounts have existed from the earliest days of pilgrimage. I am pleased to recommend it as a modern counterpart to such earlier manuals—full of penetrating insights, with welcome flashes of humour, and above all a 'snapshot' of a Land which will continue to act as a magnet to pilgrims the world over.

Andrew N. Woodsford

## Acknowledgements

The author would like to thank the Revd Andrew Woodsford, the guide on the tour, for all his help and encouragement, and his assistance with information, as well as for his meditations included in this book. He would also like to thank all who gave their views and thoughts, and his fellow members of the group.

The Bible readings are taken from the New Jerusalem Bible, published and copyright 1985 by Darton, Longman and Todd Ltd. and Doubleday & Co. Inc., and used by permission of the publishers.

On the pages of photographs, the following are by Peter Harvey: pp. 3 (top), 6 (bottom), 7 (top) and 8 (bottom).

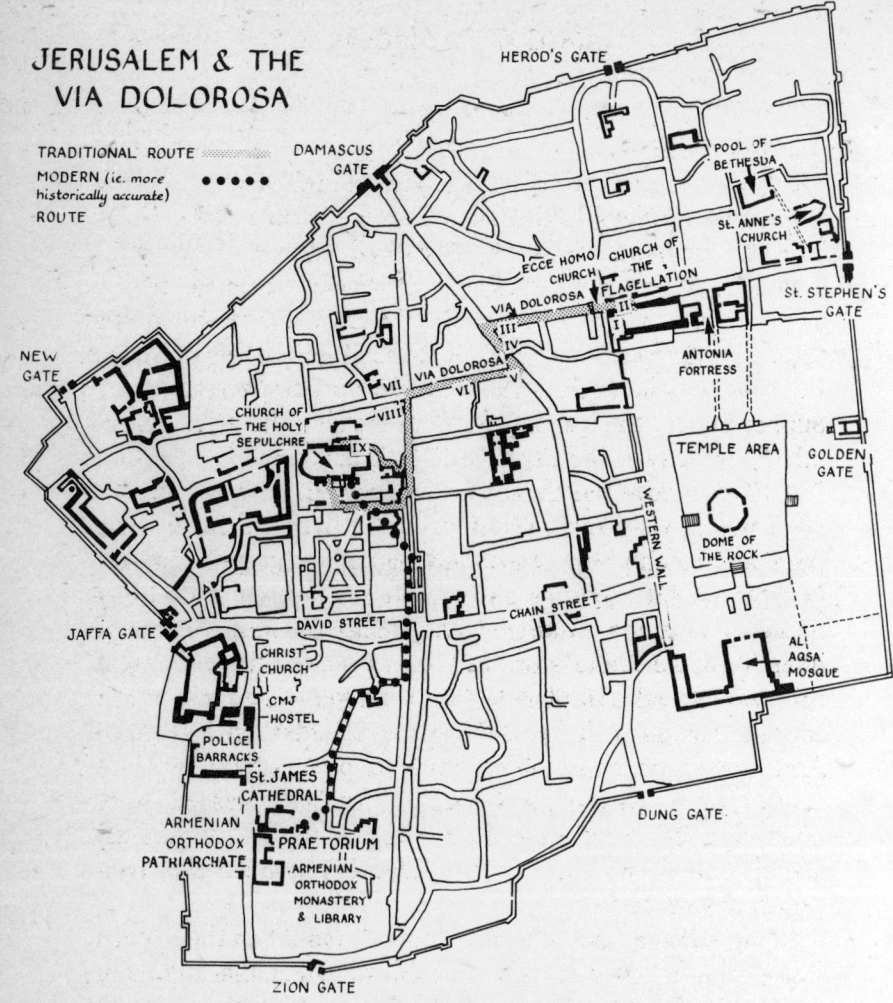

# Introduction

*A different kind of holiday*
This was not my first visit to the Holy Land. Back in 1979 I stayed in Jerusalem making programmes for BBC Radio 4. An idea had come to me, to make a series of features which could be transmitted each day during Holy Week. I chose six places or events which were of special significance in the Passion of Jesus leading up to the Crucifixion: the Mount of Olives where Jesus wept as he came into Jerusalem for Passover, the Last Supper room, the garden of Gethsemane, the trial before Pilate, the Way of the Cross, and the crucifixion on Golgotha. I was delighted when the idea was accepted. It meant that at last I was to visit this mysterious land which had for so long been very much a part of my Christian upbringing. I couldn't imagine what it would be like in reality. The only thing I had to go on were my childhood imaginings fashioned by those often repeated Bible stories: I saw Jesus in flowing white robes, the apostles similarly dressed and following him with an adoring gaze in their eyes. What did a Samaritan look like? And would there be a man rounding up passers-by to join him at his feast? And talking of feasts, how many baskets were filled with left-overs after the feeding of the five thousand? Childish questions I know, but so deeply ingrained they continued to surface.

I found accommodation at St George's Hostel on the Nablus Road, from where I set out each day to gather the sounds of the Old City and to interview as many people as possible who knew about Jerusalem and its vast, unfathomable history, reaching back thousands of years. The series was transmitted on Radio 4 as planned, repeated on the World Service as a half-hour meditation the following year on Good Friday, and then transmitted again in that form on Radio 4 the next year during Holy Week. A gratifying conclusion to a wonderful visit.

Incidentally, the English, or should I say the Anglicans, have created a perfect piece of England at St George's complete with rose garden, set in Middle Eastern surroundings. As you step through the huge entrance arch you could imagine yourself to be in Oxfordshire or Sussex. Of course Jerusalem plays host to many nationalities, all of whom have laid claim to a piece of the holy city; the Germans are there, the French, the Americans, the Scots and so on. So St George's isn't unique in that way, but it is special for other reasons. It's rather more than a place of worship for the Anglican expatriates. The compound includes a hostel, a school for Palestinian children, and St George's Ecumenical College, internationally known for its intensive Bible courses, which include geography, archaeology, liturgy and background on the life of Jesus. Some of the courses last for ten weeks and include a close look at worship in the Eastern Orthodox Churches, and study of Islam and Judaism. If you stand with your back to the Damascus Gate, on the north-west side of the Old City, the Nablus Road lies straight ahead across the main road, with Schmidt's Girls School on the corner. St George's is a ten-minute walk from there, slightly beyond the YMCA building.

My second visit to the Holy Land, which this book is about, was an organized tour with a small group of pilgrims. We were to start with a week in Jerusalem, and then move up to Galilee, which was something new for me. It struck me as curious how tours start in Jerusalem, pop into Bethlehem and Jericho and perhaps one or two other places in the area, and then move up to Galilee to where Jesus spent his childhood and most of his adult life. The chronology is upside down. However, to go first to Bethlehem, then drive some 80 miles or so north to Galilee, and then back to Jerusalem, would make neither economic nor logistical sense. It's true, you can go to the Holy Land as an individual, as I did on my first visit. But now that I've been with a qualified guide, and benefited from the experience of a local guide as well, I realize that to go alone is to miss so much. Walk down any street, go into any church, or look across to any hill or horizon, and you'll undoubtedly miss so much of significance and history right there under your nose. Much of the Jerusalem Jesus knew is now a good twenty feet below street level. A useful guide identifies and hands out the pieces of a jigsaw puzzle which you begin to fit together. Without that expertise the picture may remain confused and incomplete and that would be a pity.

We were eleven pilgrims and one British guide, Revd Andrew Woodsford: an Anglican priest, an archaeologist and a natural born teacher. Andrew is Warden of Readers for the diocese of Southwell and trained for the priesthood at Nottingham University and Cambridge. His first visit to the Holy Land was in 1964, when he and two university friends drove to Jerusalem in a Land Rover, worked on an archaeological dig for two months, and drove back again. He made his second trip two years later and spent six months working at the British School of Archaeology in Jerusalem, tutored by the renowned Dame Kathleen Kenyon. She was Principal of St Hugh's College, Oxford, and a student of the famous Sir Mortimer Wheeler of TV's *Animal, Vegetable, Mineral* in the 1950s. Kathleen Kenyon's first dig was at Jericho about the same time as Sir Mortimer was dazzling viewers with his vast and detailed knowledge of everything to do with the ancient world. In the 1960s Dr Kenyon excavated the ancient city of David on the south-east ridge of Jerusalem, the exact location of which was unknown until she came on the scene. Under this sort of tutelage at the British School, where it was 'dig-talk' for breakfast, lunch and dinner, Andrew learned his craft.

Is archaeology for those who prefer to live in the past, and reject their present surroundings? Not according to Andrew. For him it's finding out about people in the past, the details of how they lived, what they ate, what they worked at, and how they spent their time. That knowledge then helps put the Bible into context, making its interpretation more accurate. Whilst the Bible is true for all time, if it isn't earthed in a particular period of history, there is a risk it will be misunderstood. Andrew's priestly theology and his interest in archaeology complement each other perfectly. Add to that his constant enthusiasm and you have an invaluable guide.

What, then, does the average Christian gain from a pilgrimage which takes in all the holy places?

One of the early Church Fathers said that the Holy Land itself is the fifth gospel. We have the four written gospels of Matthew, Mark, Luke and John; but following in the steps of Jesus is really like another gospel in action, rather than in words. To walk down a street in Jerusalem or to pass by a place and to be able to say 'over there is the village of Nain', to identify everyday locations that Jesus and his followers were familiar with, gives the pilgrim a sense of enrichment each time he or she hears a particular passage from the Bible. If you hear the story of the Transfiguration in the New Testament, and you've actually been on Mount Tabor, and seen the view over Galilee, then that story becomes more significant. Imagine following the Via Dolorosa when all the shops are open, and the bartering is going on as it does on most days. It's probably reminiscent of the first Good Friday. You'll discover also in the Holy Land that all the holy places are marked and built over by churches, some of them attractive, some not so pleasing. At first that can be something of a disappointment. In the West we like to see things as they were, untouched and in their original state. But don't forget, in many instances the early Christians built small churches over areas which meant something to them and their faith. They had a reason for doing it, probably the same reason why we visit them today. These churches can serve the modern pilgrim in two ways: they help to establish the authenticity of the site, and it's inspiring to know that Christian worship has been continuing there sometimes for as long as 1800 years. To hear words of Scripture read out where prayers have been said for so many centuries is a very moving experience.

From the very outset, a trip to the Holy Land is different from any other trip you've been on. The first hint of that is when you arrive at the airport and discover that you seem to be getting VIP treatment; all El Al passengers are herded through special departure gates, through special security systems, including baggage and body checks. You'll still have your large luggage with you; so make sure you have a trolley if your cases are heavy. It can be a long walk to the departure lounge. Once there, the whole experience becomes very different.

Each passenger is questioned in detail about luggage: Who packed it? Did anyone give you any object which you haven't examined? Has anyone had access to your luggage since you packed it? And so on. Then the really tricky bit: Have you been to Israel before? Do you know anyone in Israel? Do you know any Arabs? If so, who are they and what was your business with them? This line of questioning can go on for fifteen minutes, including if necessary a detailed examination of all luggage. Your passport and airline ticket will be carefully scrutinized before you are eventually cleared to board the plane. The process is unusual and can be something of an ordeal, but according to the Israelis, there's good reason for it. El Al (Hebrew for 'to the skies') Airlines are extremely security conscious because of threats to their national security from neighbouring Arab countries. It's true that on one or two occasions El Al aircraft were hijacked in the past, in the late 1960s and early 1970s. But since then, the airline claims to be the safest in the world with a record second to none. To maintain that record, the security is the tightest in the world. All those who scrutinize passengers and luggage are Israeli citizens, normally young graduates of either sex who have also done their compulsory three-year military service. They are dedicated people who do one or two-year stints before returning to Israel to begin a career. In Britain El Al runs services from both Manchester and Newcastle, and even security for these flights is supervised by young Israelis who fly up there to do their job. This vast security operation, duplicated all over the world wherever El Al flies, costs millions of pounds, but they think it's worth it. It's also good to know, that once aboard, you're probably safer than on any other airline. On our particular flight, many of the passengers were Hasidic Jews, the men in their characteristic black clothes, tall hats, and ringlets curling down in front of their ears; the womenfolk, not quite as distinctive as the men, favour plain long dresses or skirts and often wear headscarves. These are orthodox Jews who succeed in living a strict Jewish way of life—to the very letter of the law. The Hebrew word *hasid* means 'one who is pious', and to demonstrate that virtue, early in the flight some 50 or 60 black-clad, bearded figures threaded their way to the rear of the aircraft and began to pray with a curious swaying movement. Thankfully such uneven distribution of weight did nothing to hamper the progress of the Boeing 747; and four hours later we landed at Ben Gurion Airport on time, at midnight and in balmy November weather. We had arrived in the Holy Land and our pilgrimage proper was about to begin.

# DAY 1

## Jerusalem and Bethlehem

Jerusalem time is two hours ahead of GMT, which meant we arrived at 2.00 a.m. local time. It was warm but raining as the coach sped the 45-minute journey from Tel Aviv Airport to Jerusalem. We checked in at the Notre Dame Centre, situated opposite the New Gate on the north-western corner of the Old City. It's a beautifully restored pilgrim centre owned by the Vatican and perfectly placed for access to the holy places. Within ten minutes you could be at the church of the Holy Sepulchre.

The next morning, after a self-service breakfast of boiled eggs, fresh fruit and bread (never any fresh orange juice in this land of the Jaffas), our coach arrived at 9 o'clock and we set off on our first day of exploration. If you look at a map of the Old City (an essential item which will become your intimate friend) you'll see it has eight gates, all of which give access to different areas. Starting with Herod's Gate on the north side, and moving in a clockwise direction there's St Stephen's (or Lion's) Gate, Golden (or Beautiful) Gate (sealed up in 1542 by Suleiman the Magnificent because it was near to the Muslim burial ground), Dung Gate, Zion Gate, Jaffa Gate, New Gate and Damascus Gate. Within ten minutes we were at the Dung Gate on the south side of the city, and there we were joined by our Arab guide, David (Daoud) Abasi, who was to be with us almost every day. David turned out to be a very amusing and knowledgeable character and we enjoyed having him around. He invariably had a joyous welcome for us when we met—always dead on time and very smartly dressed.

David was as thin as a rake, and liked his cigarettes. His Arab lineage, of which he was very proud, had bestowed on him a magnificent semitic nose. David's family tree could be traced back 900 years in Jerusalem, 'the city of prophets, the city of peace' as he put it. His father had joined the Jordanian Army and became a general under King Hussein. David was an only child and when he was only a few months old, his father died. According to Muslim practice, any brother of the deceased is expected to marry his widow and assume all responsibilities, including the upbringing of any children. Thus David's uncle, who served in the British Police Force during the British Mandate in Palestine, became his stepfather. As a young man David joined the TJFF, the Trans-Jordan Frontier Forces, on the Jordan side. Three years later he joined the RAF until the end of the Second World War. After that he worked for BOAC—now part of British Airways. David became a tourist guide in 1967, and since that time he has loved his job of showing Christians around the holy places. Like all Palestinians I met, David was very depressed about the prospects for the future of Palestinian Arabs, although he always spoke in a conciliatory manner of both Jews and Arabs. He had sent his three sons abroad for a 'decent education'—not available, he said, to Palestinians in Israel—and they all settled in the United States. He told me how much he misses them. Now in his 70s, David lamented the fact that no guides, other than Jewish, have been appointed since 1975. David's parade-ground manner and his foghorn voice, doubtless a legacy from his RAF days, were extremely useful for rounding up wayward pilgrims and making them listen to what he was saying!

## Dung Gate

Its real name in Arabic is Bab al-Maghariba (Gate of the Moors) because of the North Africans who lived there from the sixteenth century. From here, on the south side of the city, the Roman-Byzantine Cardo Maximus began and continued through the centre of the city to the north side as far as the Damascus Gate. This was a colonnaded shopping mall effectively dividing the city into two parts. Outside the Dung Gate, to the south-east, is the spring of Gihon (or spring of the Virgin Mary). This was the main ancient water supply to the city, and when King David decided to make Jerusalem his capital around 1000 BC his troops used the man-made shaft at the spring to pass under the city walls. At that time Jerusalem was very small; even in the time of Jesus, ten centuries later, the total population was only 15,000: large enough then for a capital city, but small by modern standards. That statistic began to give me some idea of the reduced scale of things we were to meet as our pilgrimage progressed. The city walls, as you see them now, are not very old in Holy Land terms. They were built about 450 years ago by Suleiman the Magnificent. He built the present Old City above the one the Crusaders built in the twelfth century. It's estimated that throughout the course of history, Jerusalem has been built over seven or eight times. Clearing away and excavating is an expensive business, so the cheapest and quickest method was to rebuild the new on the rubble of the old.

## The Wailing Wall

Under a clear blue November sky, and in a comfortable temperature of 70° F, we strolled north-west for ten minutes and came to the Wailing Wall (or Western Wall to be accurate) below the Dome of the Rock mosque, whose massive golden dome (which catches the morning and the evening sun) dominates the whole of the Jerusalem landscape. Between the Western Wall and the dome is the other major mosque, Al Aqsa. Two holy places for Muslims adjacent to the holy place for Jews. The approach to the wall is across a very large open square, and as you draw closer a remarkable sight unfolds. On most days—except the Sabbath—possibly hundreds of Jews pray facing the massive stone slabs of Herod's wall. The longer section is reserved for men, who stand inches from the granite slabs and rock to and fro whilst they sing (or wail) their prayers from the Torah. The women's section is over to the right. The whole area is a sensitive one, so you can expect a heavy military presence at all entry points. Bags and personal effects are subject to search and scrutiny by armed Israeli patrols before you are allowed to approach the wall. It's something you quickly become accustomed to, more so in Jerusalem that in other areas of the Holy Land. But once past the guards, the atmosphere is quite relaxed. The niches in the magnificent and beautifully built wall are stuffed with rolled and folded pieces of paper, all containing prayers and petitions. The tradition of praying at the wall goes back to the destruction of the Temple in AD 70. Four years before that date, the Jews rose up against the Roman occupation (the First Revolt), and the city and the Temple were destroyed in reprisal. Jews at the wall still pray in lamentation of that destruction. If you can get near to the wall, the wailing sounds very genuine and heartfelt. I stood near to an old woman who really did wail as though she was at a funeral. It was a strange and haunting experience. You can almost feel the antiquity in the atmosphere.

### *The Golden Gate*

We skirted round the south-east corner of the Temple Mount and came to the Golden Gate, on the east side of the city, which is referred to in the Acts of the Apostles as the Beautiful Gate (Acts 3:10). It was the occasion when Peter and John came to the Temple to pray and were stopped by a lame beggar. Peter told him he had no money to give; 'But I will give you what I have: in the name of Jesus Christ the Nazarene, walk!' The lame man stood up and walked. Peter then rounded on the amazed onlookers, scolding them for being so surprised at something he had done in the name of Jesus. During the Crusader period the gate was opened twice a year for solemn processions on Palm Sunday and the feast of the Exaltation of the Cross. Since then it has been closed. This was the entrance Jesus came through to go to the Temple to drive out the money-changers. Nowadays, the Palm Sunday procession comes down from the Mount of Olives opposite, across the Kidron valley, and then it has to go a little north, through St Stephen's Gate, to pass through the city walls.

At this point David, our Arab guide, told one of his many jokes. It was about the friends of a recently deceased man who decided to make a posthumous collection for him. When a rich friend heard of this, he promised to double the amount raised. Eventually a very respectable sum resulted and it was taken to the rich friend. He expressed satisfaction, promptly wrote out a cheque to the dead man for double the amount, placed it on the coffin and made off with the cash! David laughed loudest and longest, but we all joined in.

## Dome of the Rock

A thousand years before Jesus was born, King David brought a threshing floor to accommodate the Ark of the Covenant, the symbol of God's protection of the chosen people and religious focal point for the whole Jewish nation. Later his son Solomon built the first Temple here, which was destroyed in the sixth century BC by the Babylonians. The second Temple was erected 70 years later. Only a few years before Christ was born, Herod the Great (37–4 BC) decided to please the Jews and enlarge the whole area: to a staggering 30 acres. He built huge retaining walls (of which the Wailing Wall is one) to shore up the flat expanse and adorned the area with balconies, covered galleries, colonnades and grand staircases. It must have been a magnificent affair. When Jesus knew it, the work was still in progress. One wonders if he ever remarked on the noise of the workmen on the building-site as he tried to preach above the din. Along with the rest of Jerusalem, it was destroyed in AD 70 by the emperor's son Titus, but the immovable, slab-sided foundations remain to this day. During Byzantine times the Temple area was neglected and used as a rubbish dump. In the seventh century the holy city fell to the forces of Islam who built Al Aqsa and then the Dome on this once Jewish Temple site. According to Muslim teaching, the prophet Muhammad was taken up to heaven from the rock which the dome covers, where he received the Holy Quran. Sixty years after his death, the mosque was built to commemorate this event. After Mecca and Medina, it is the holiest place to all Muslims. When the Crusaders ousted the Muslims in the twelfth and thirteenth centuries, the Dome and Al Aqsa mosque nearby were turned into a church and a Crusader palace respectively. Both places reverted to Islam when the Crusaders were beaten back.

You have to divest yourself of shoes, handbags, cameras and any other tourist paraphernalia before being allowed to enter the Dome of the Rock. Once inside, the architecture is breathtaking in its symmetry and simplicity. As on the outside, the walls are covered in intricate and perfectly designed ceramic mosaics, and the mosque within a mosque in the centre houses the rock itself. Muslims also believe this was the place where Abraham was ready to slay his beloved son Isaac. Abraham is a prophet revered by Muslims—as is Jesus. David our guide was very proud of the mosque and showed us around with great enthusiasm, noting particularly the huge inside of the aluminium dome immediately above the rock, which weighs a mere 35 tons—unlike the previous one made of lead which weighed 200 tons. Down the centuries the Dome has been renovated countless times, and as recently as the 1960s a lot of restoration work has been done to maintain the obviously high standard of preservation and sheer architectural beauty.

### *Al Aqsa Mosque*

This must be one of the largest, and longest, mosques you're ever likely to enter. Carpets scattered one on top of another cover the whole of the floor area, and two great armies of marble columns (donated by Mussolini) march the full length of the interior. David was at pains to tell us of the fire started in 1969 by a mentally disturbed Australian which did considerable damage to the painted ceiling at the far end, and also destroyed the cedar-wood pulpit given by Saladin in 1187. Repair work is taking years to complete.

## *Bethlehem* (*House of Bread*)

Five miles to the south of Jerusalem, on the Hebron Road, is Bethlehem. Frankly, these days, the birthplace of Jesus can be a disappointment. Nowhere is there a more tense area, alive with armed militia and an air of menace and potential danger. But nevertheless, groups like ours simply press on and visit these places, and nine times out of ten there's no problem. Occasionally, when there is a fracas, tourists are instructed not to go. For example, we were scheduled to visit the Shepherds' Fields, but because of Palestinian stone-throwing, we had to give it a miss.

We arrived in the afternoon at a deserted Manger Square which is in front of the basilica of the Nativity. In days gone by, after a morning's trading, the shops and markets in Bethlehem and Jerusalem closed around midday and reopened in the late afternoon for the evening. But now, because of the *intifada*, everything closes at midday and remains so until the following morning. I'm afraid without the hustle and bustle of market traders and the people buying and selling, the colour and atmosphere of the place is missing. But don't be put off visiting Bethlehem. There are fascinating things to see, and it's as good a place as any to feel the authenticity of the Holy Land.

According to biblical scholar Fr Jerome Murphy-O'Connor (the Dominican priest and vice-director at the École Biblique et Archéologique Française), Mary and Joseph were born in Bethlehem and they moved to Nazareth because of Herod's unhealthy interest in their child 'born to be king of the Jews' (Matthew 2). Herod asked the chief priests where the Messiah would be born; 'in Bethlehem of Judaea' was the reply. On Herod's instructions men went to Bethlehem to seek out Jesus, but they were too late. The Holy Family had fled to Egypt, and later when Herod died, they moved north to

Nazareth in Galilee. So (according to Fr Murphy-O'Connor) Luke—who imagined Mary and Joseph were from Nazareth because they spent so much of their lives there—is wrong when he writes that Mary and Joseph came down from Galilee for Emperor Augustus's census. They were already there. Where this piece of New Testament erudition leaves all the struggling infant school teachers throughout the Christian world, preparing the children for their nativity plays each Christmas, is hard to imagine. Perhaps celebrating in the traditional and spiritual way is just as important as historical accuracy.

Our tiny band approached the basilica of the Nativity at the east end of Manger Square, to be met by a group of rather bored-looking touts who proffered rosary beads, postcards, silver jewellery and shepherds' pipes. You'll find this sort of slightly irritating pressure mainly in and around Jerusalem, but in a sense you can't blame the Palestinians for wanting to earn a living. Outside the capital the hard sell doesn't exist. So, buy something if you must, and pass through the tiny door in the Crusader façade into the rather dark and gloomy cavern of the Basilica. Helena (255–330), the mother of the Emperor Constantine, was traditionally the first Christian pilgrim and it was Constantine who built the first church on this site in the fourth century. St Jerome (342–420) spent over 30 years of his life here, in a basement stone cell, translating the Bible from Hebrew and Greek into Latin—the Vulgate as it was called—to make it accessible to more people.

In the sixth century the Emperor Justinian ordered the small church at Bethlehem pulled down and a much larger one built 'of such splendour, size and beauty that none even in the Holy Land should surpass it'. Apart from the fifteenth-century roof (made from pine donated by Philip of Burgundy and lead donated by Edward IV) and the floor, the church is much the same now as it was in the sixth century. Some remnants of Crusader wall-paintings are still visible above the massive pillars which flank the nave and lead to the high altar. Don't miss the trapdoor towards the centre of the nave; through it you can see a few square feet of beautiful but rather dusty Byzantine mosaic which covers the entire basilica floor underneath the existing floor. It makes you wonder for a moment what Constantine's original building must have been like. Andrew told us a charming story of a mosaic, now no more, which used to be on the inside wall above the main entrance. In 614 the Persian invasion destroyed all the churches in the region except for this one. During the sack the soldiers came in through the door and saw the picture on the wall of the three wise men, the Magi, who were depicted in Persian costume. Impressed and flattered by this illustration, the soldiers rode away and the church was spared.

At almost any time of the day, some service or other will be in progress in the basilica. Part of the reason is that the church is occupied by three branches of the Christian Church: the Franciscan Order, the Latin rite keepers of the holy places, who occupy the church of St Catherine of Alexandria, connected with the main church; the Armenians; and the Greek Orthodox who actually own it. Next door in St Catherine's, the friars were singing vespers, and in the basilica the Armenians were having their ceremony at their side altar. At the Greek (main) altar three monks were singing their office by candlelight. Here candles burn everywhere before altars, icons and statues; priests flit from place to place in strange robes and the air is filled with the smell of burning wax and incense, and chanting in three ancient tongues. The magic begins to take hold. That early Christians began to pray and worship on this spot within a very few years of Jesus' crucifixion is an impressive thought.

Through the gloom we made our way to the right of the Greek high altar, away from the liturgical muddle, and descended down narrow Crusader steps hewn from solid rock, into the grotto or chamber said to be the birth place of Jesus. It's a small space, inevitably crowded with pilgrims and visitors who pass through in an endless stream to catch a quick glimpse of the spot, marked with a large silver star set into the paving. We gathered round in a tight space a little away from the tiny cavern with the star, and Andrew read an extract from the gospel according to Matthew.

MATTHEW 2:1–12

After Jesus had been born at Bethlehem in Judaea during the reign of King Herod, suddenly some wise men came to Jerusalem from the east asking, 'Where is the infant king of the Jews? We saw his star as it rose and have come to do him homage.' When King Herod heard this he was perturbed and so was the whole of Jerusalem. He called together all the chief priests and the scribes of the people, and enquired of them where the Christ was to be born. They told him, 'At Bethlehem in Judaea, for this is what the prophet wrote:

And you, Bethlehem, in the land of Judah,
you are by no means the least among the leaders of Judah,
for from you will come a leader who will shepherd my people
  Israel.'

Then Herod summoned the wise men to see him privately. He asked them the exact date on which the star had appeared and sent them on to Bethlehem with the words,'Go and find out all about the child, and when you have found him, let me know, so that I too may go and do him homage.' Having listened to what the king had to say, they set out. And suddenly the star they had seen rising went forward and halted over the place where the child was. The sight of the star filled them with delight, and going into the house they saw the child with his mother Mary, and falling to their knees they did him homage. Then, opening their treasures, they offered him gifts of gold and frankincense and myrrh. But they were given a warning in a dream not to go back to Herod, and returned to their own country by a different way.

*'Hic de virgine Maria Jesus Christus natus est.'*
*(Here Jesus Christ was born of the Virgin Mary.)*
*Here?*
*A silver star.*
*A marble floor.*
*All the ornate trappings of a splendid ritual.*
*Nothing could be further from your humble beginnings:*
*a stinking manger*

*amid the cattle.*
*No room at the inn.*
*It is not easy to imagine all this today,*
*especially here.*
*Yet we bow in worship*
*and adore.*

*You became man, Lord,*
*for us,*
*for me.*
*That means you know just what it's like*
*to be born in a stinking cave,*
*to grow up in a humble home,*
*to die prematurely after great suffering.*
*None of this would have been possible*
*if it wasn't for Bethlehem.*
*Here.*
*Here you were born.*
*Here it all began.*
*Here let me begin again.*
*Here Jesus Christ is born—again.*
*Be born again in me.*

O God, we thank you for the message of peace that Christmas brings to our distracted world. Give peace among the nations, peace in the Holy Land, peace in our homes, and peace in our hearts as we remember at Bethlehem the birth of the Prince of Peace, Jesus Christ our Lord. Amen.

Adapted from *Worship Now*

So here was the cave where Jesus was born, a simple cavern hollowed out at one end of this tiny chamber. It wasn't so unusual to be born in a cave in those days: most poor households had one for the cattle to use. When you travel from Jerusalem to Bethlehem, you see many houses that are just a room or crude shack built in front of a cave. What could have been more natural than for Mary to retire into the back room to give birth to her child? The Latin inscription on the floor near to the star reads 'Here Jesus Christ was born of the Virgin Mary'. This spot has been venerated by millions of Christians down the ages.

The cave was damaged by fire just over a century ago, and the furnishings are relatively modern. Large sheets of leather drape the walls, with asbestos underneath as a precaution against further disaster; but oil-lamps still burn before the grotto. It's hot, it's stuffy, and if (in spite of all that distraction) you can really appreciate where you are and what it means, it's very heady stuff. Most scholars and historians agree that this really is the place of the Nativity; prophecies were made in the Old Testament about Bethlehem as the place from which a ruler of Israel would emerge; it was also known as King David's place of birth; and it was always a small village, thereby reducing any confusion of location. Add to that the powerful witness of continuous veneration down the centuries, and you have a site and a tradition which is more than likely 100 per cent accurate.

The church of St Catherine is about a hundred years old—light, airy and pleasant. I spoke to one of the American friars, who'd been in the Holy Land for 28 years. The Franciscans have been in Bethlehem, and other holy places, for almost 700 years—almost back to the time of St Francis himself. You'll soon become familiar with their simple brown tunics, white rope girdles and open sandals. They look after many of the major shrines and act as well-informed guides in most areas. The friar didn't wish to give his name for fear of upsetting the 'authorities' who might deport him if he criticized local politics. He described for me how it was at Christmas here—celebrations televised to many countries every Christmas Eve. In reality there are three separate celebrations of Christmas: Latin, Greek Orthodox and Armenian. All follow different liturgical calendars from 25 December into January. The friar was saddened by the fact that over recent years hardly any visitors have come to Midnight Mass because of the political tension. But the full liturgy proceeds just the same. He assured me he still looks forward to Christmas here as though it were his very first!

Time to pile back into the bus and head for home as the first day drew to a close. On the way back to Jerusalem, we were 'guided' into a large shop and encouraged to buy the usual array of Holy Land trinkets: statues in olive wood, ashtrays bearing various crests, rosary beads and brass coffee-pots. Tourism is down in the Holy Land since the *intifada*, and therefore there is greater pressure to sell to those who do come. As in all tourist areas wherever you are, the souvenirs and trinkets soon all begin to look the same, probably because they are all the same. As you'll discover, some prices are fairer than others. I decided those shops directly attached to churches gave the best value and quality.

As we approached the city, there was still an hour of light left (darkness falls very quickly at around six in the autumn), so we decided to leave the bus at the Jaffa Gate and stroll through the Old City before returning to Notre Dame. We walked through the suq, the markets running through the cavernous narrow streets, usually so noisy and busy, but at this time of day deserted because of the midday strike. Eventually we did come upon an area where activity had not yet ceased, the Cardo Maximus. Some of the tastefully converted, trendy shops were still open and doing a little business. By contrast with the suq, it's light, fresh, and the antique shops and artists' studios give the unmistakable impression of being very expensive. On one of the walls there's a facsimile of an ancient map of the Cardo in mosaic. It's a rather beautiful piece of work and not to be missed. You can buy a copy on a postcard. From a distance it could almost be mistaken for the London Underground map!

# DAY 2

# Bethany, Jericho, Masada and the Dead Sea

After dinner at the end of the first day, most people went straight to bed. Not only had we made the journey by air to the Holy Land the day before, but we'd had a very busy and packed first day, which included parts of the Old City and a trip down to Bethlehem. We were also getting to know each other quite quickly, because as a group you spend a good deal of your time together every day.

At 8.30 next morning, after a self-service breakfast, we were all set to leave. The sun was shining as usual, the temperature was pleasantly warm, and our bus pulled out of the centre's gates, turned left down the hill past the Damascus Gate and headed east along the road to Jericho and to Bethany.

## Bethany

This is the village, only two miles from Jerusalem, where Jesus' friends Martha, Mary and Lazarus lived.

JOHN 11:1-3

There was a man named Lazarus of Bethany, the village of Mary and her sister, Martha, and he was ill. It was the same Mary, the sister of the sick man Lazarus, who anointed the Lord with ointment and wiped his feet with her hair. The sisters sent this message to Jesus, 'Lord, the man you love is ill.'

The original church of Lazarus was built in the fourth century by early Christians to commemorate one of Jesus' greatest miracles: the raising of Lazarus from the dead. Some original mosaics can still be seen in the floor. The first church was destroyed by the Persians in the early seventh century and restored by the Crusaders in the eleventh century. The present church was built by the Franciscans in the 1950s on top of the Crusader foundations. As you'd expect, all the artwork, stained glass and pictures inside this attractive church illustrate in different ways how Lazarus was raised from his tomb. However, at this point, Andrew decided to read a passage from Luke relating another more domestic matter which arose out of one of Jesus' visits to his friends' house at Bethany.

Luke 10:38–42

In the course of their journey he came to a village, and a woman named Martha welcomed him into her house. She had a sister called Mary, who sat down at the Lord's feet and listened to him speaking. Now Martha who was distracted with all the serving, came to him and said, 'Lord, do you not care that my sister is leaving me to do the serving all by myself? Please tell her to help me.' But the Lord answered, 'Martha, Martha,' he said, 'you worry and you fret about so many things, and yet few are needed, indeed only one. It is Mary who has chosen the better part, and it is not to be taken from her.'

Under the church is an olive press, very similar to the one that would have been in the garden of Gethsemane in Jesus' time. It's a crude contraption of a wooden harness, a huge stone base where ripe olives would have been spread and a massive, solid stone wheel slowly pulled round over them by a donkey or camel. The oil yielded up was collected through a small draining hole in the centre of the stone base. David, our Arab guide, told us it was in use until very recently.

The tomb of Lazarus is just a little way from the church. A lady keeper was on duty, and spoke for three minutes flat about the fact that this was the tomb of Lazarus. She spoke parrot-fashion and probably didn't understand what she was saying. None of us did. We descended a cold and damp flight of stone steps very carefully, and saw the place where Lazarus came out. Originally it was at ground level, but the new entrance is up a slight incline and therefore higher than the tomb itself. One of the sentences I did manage to catch from the lady keeper, as she tore into her set-piece explanation, was that the Crusaders were so taken with Lazarus's resurrection story that they brought his remains to France. A short time previously in the church, David had said that after being resurrected from the dead Lazarus lived another 40 years and ended up in Marseilles in the south of France. It's a story I've never heard before. But David had another surprise in store. As we gathered at the bottom of the staircase in Lazarus's tomb and tried to absorb the significance of what we were seeing, suddenly the sound of a booming voice came rushing down into the stone chamber: 'Lazarus, come forth!' For a split second we all stood still and stared at each other in surprise. Then we realized it was David who was bawling out from the head of the staircase and frightening us all to death! It turned out to be a very amusing moment.

Leaving Bethany, we then pressed on to Jericho, about twenty miles north-east of Jerusalem in the Jordan valley. It's a lonely road through the Judaean desert with little traffic and nothing much to see but barren hills in every direction. We spotted the odd bedouin shepherd on horseback with his goats and sheep. We stopped by the roadside, and Andrew pointed to a distant cliff face: and there, clinging to the side of the Wadi Qilt, was the Greek Orthodox monastery of St George Koziba, which seemed to be in the middle of nowhere. You can walk there in 40 minutes if you have the time (which we didn't) but I must say I was drawn to it, and some of us would have liked to have seen the monastery at closer quarters. Visitors are very welcome. In Byzantine times there were over 100 monasteries in this area, but few remain. The monks used to give water to pilgrims on their way from Jerusalem to Jericho—probably a good day's journey. Hermits first came to this site in the fifth century and it became a monastery some years later. Some of the hermitages are still in use. The present-day construction is very modern, and was finished in 1901. There are lots of biblical legends attached to this monastery: Elijah stayed here (1 Kings 17:3) and was fed by ravens; and Joachim was told that his wife Anne would bear the Virgin Mary.

### Jericho *(City of Palm Trees)*

The city is about 24 miles north-east of Jerusalem. Leaving Bethany, we pressed on; and suddenly, round a bend in the desert landscape, we saw Jericho. It was a wonderful moment to see this vast and green oasis, its palm trees and cultivated fields of fruit and vegetables, quite out of context with the surrounding barren hills and valleys. Its secret of course is water. There are seven fresh-water springs dotted around the Jericho valley, the main one being Elisha's Spring (named after Elisha in the Old Testament who threw salt into the springs to purify them after they had become sour). These sources provide fresh water the whole year round.

The main reference to Jericho in the Old Testament is in chapter 6 of the book of Joshua, whose troops captured it from the Canaanites by marching around the walls once a day for six days. On the seventh day the priests blew their trumpets, and as the people shouted 'The Lord has put the city in our power' the walls came tumbling down! Thus Joshua took Jericho: a great prize because of its situation and fertile locality. The Jericho Joshua would have known is not the modern city we see today; the Old Testament Jericho can only be imagined because it's under a ruin-mound, or *tel*, on the east side. The observation platforms overlooking the *tel* give a fine panoramic view of Jericho in all its lush greenery.

As we gathered on the platform, Andrew really came into his stride. As an archaeologist and a great Holy Land enthusiast, he began to tell us about this very important find made this century, which confirmed that this *tel* represented the oldest city in existence—over 8,000 years ago. Apparently before Dame Kathleen Kenyon's excavations no one had realized that man had organized himself into walled cities so many thousands of years ago. What we were actually looking at was a partly exposed pile of stones built in a rough circular shape which vaguely represented a watch-tower. Our platform was on the inside of the ancient city. Twenty or thirty years ago it was possible, on this site, to see very clearly about seventeen levels of occupation reaching back 8,000 years and coming up to the Iron Age period (1350–722 BC) during which Joshua and the Israelites arrived. Weathering since the excavations has more or less obscured the various time-layers.

By New Testament times this *tel* was completely deserted and Jericho had shifted back along the Wadi Qilt to a site we passed on our way into Jericho from Bethany. (Incidentally, King Herod had a winter palace at Jericho, which enjoys a moderate temperature all the year round. He also built a theatre for his guests' entertainment.) Looking at it from a strictly archaeological point of view, Andrew raised a doubt about the authenticity of this *tel*; nowhere—apart from one small fireplace in a house—has anything yet been found that can definitely be dated back to the period at which Joshua is supposed to have conquered the city. There is the possibility that the 'walls-came-tumbling-down' story may have occurred at a nearby settlement, and not at Jericho at all. In later years the story-tellers attached the incident to Jericho simply because it was the largest and most important city of the time. Books, which often indicate the walls of the *tel* and claim that these are the walls of Jericho, are not necessarily accurate. The true story of what happened when the people shouted at the walls, and precisely which walls they were, may have to remain a mystery buried deep in the Old Testament for ever.

When the Crusaders left the Holy Land in the twelfth century, Jericho declined into little more than a village, and revived only this century and developed into the fruit-producing area it is today. Looking out over Jericho you are looking at the occupied West Bank which was taken from Jordan in the 1967 War. This fertile piece of land stretches as far east as the river Jordan, now the border between Jordan and Israel. Fruit and vegetable lorries, laden with Jericho produce, make daily journeys across the Allenby Bridge into Jordan and on to

Amman. The Jericho region is fertile and therefore a valuable piece of territory; and wars have always been about territory. Our timetable didn't permit us to linger in Jericho itself, although I was greatly attracted to it. We caught only a glimpse of the city as we drove through on the way to Masada. Jericho was the place where Jesus healed Bartimaeus of his blindness:

Mark 10:46–52

They reached Jericho; and as he left Jericho with his disciples and a great crowd, Bartimaeus—that is, the son of Timaeus—a blind beggar, was sitting at the side of the road. When he heard that it was Jesus of Nazareth, be began to shout and to cry out, 'Son of David, Jesus, have pity on me.' And many of them scolded him and told him to keep quiet, but he only shouted all the louder, 'Son of David, have pity on me.' Jesus stopped and said, 'Call him here.' So they called the blind man over. 'Courage', they said, 'get up; he is calling you.' So throwing off his cloak, he jumped up and went to Jesus. Then Jesus spoke, 'What do you want me to do for you?' The blind man said to him, 'Rabbuni, let me see again.' Jesus said to him, 'Go; your faith has saved you.' And at once his sight returned and he followed him along the road.

Andrew drew our attention to a tree by the roadside; tradition has it that this sycamore tree was the one Zacchaeus, the chief tax-collector, climbed to catch a better view of Jesus as he made his way through the city, surrounded as usual by lots of people. Zacchaeus's efforts were well rewarded according to Luke.

Luke 19:1–10

He entered Jericho and was going through the town and suddenly a man whose name was Zacchaeus made his appearance; he was one of the senior tax-collectors and a wealthy man. He kept trying to see which Jesus was, but he was too short and could not see him for the crowd; so he ran ahead and climbed a sycamore tree to catch a glimpse of Jesus who was to pass that way. When Jesus reached the spot he looked up and spoke to him, 'Zacchaeus, come down. Hurry, because I am to stay at your house today. And he hurried down and welcomed him joyfully.

It's a very warm, human story, and no doubt Zacchaeus dined out on it for the rest of his life! Both at the *tel* car park, and driving through the city, there's plenty of opportunity to sample the wonderful fruit of the area. Curiously, the skins of the oranges are green, and the flesh quite pale; but the taste is excellent.

## Masada

Out of Jericho, we travelled due south and soon came to the northern shores of the Dead Sea. We sped down the west side of the sea, which is actually a great lake. Andrew mentioned that since he was first here in the 1960s the water line has receded considerably because the sea has begun to evaporate. Masada itself is a huge natural granite fortress; it stands guard by the Dead Sea shore, and broods over sad and terrible memories. It's more a place of pilgrimage for Jews than for Christians because of what took place here 2,000 years ago. The site wasn't discovered until 1850 by British explorers and excavated only in the 1960s, by hundreds of Jewish volunteers. It's now a symbol to the Jewish people of the weak against the strong—how a stand can be made against the oppressor, although in this case the ultimate price had to be paid for victory.

It was one of King Herod's summer palaces, similar to the one at Jericho. It was in fact his bolt-hole should the Jews turn against him. Masada was a daring and ambitious plan to make an oasis on a rock in one of the harshest climates in the world. Somehow Herod, his architects and engineers made it work. To make it self-contained he built cisterns to catch rain water in the wet season. Enough water was gathered each year to facilitate a swimming pool, a bathhouse and saunas. A palace occupied a position over at the western side, and you can still see fine mosaics which decorated this opulent palace. Not content with that, he constructed a villa on the north face to catch the coolest winds. When he died the Romans took Masada in 4 BC and made it into a garrison. In AD 66 the Jews revolted against the Roman occupiers and the Zealots came by night to Masada, slaughtered the Roman soldiers and made it the headquarters. From there, this guerrilla force or first-century freedom fighters (depending on which side you favoured) played havoc with the Romans, and it fell to the lot of General Flavius Silva and the 15,000 men of the Tenth Legion to deal with Masada. In AD 72 he built a permanent camp and a siege wall around the rock—the outlines of which are remarkably visible from the fortress top. After three long years of siege, the Romans had constructed a ramp to breach the western walls and the Zealots eventually realized they were beaten. Ironically most of the Roman labour to build the ramp was provided by Jewish slaves, captured probably in Jerusalem during the revolt a few years earlier. But rather than surrender to the enemy, the Zealots embarked upon a course of action which has secured the fame of Masada forever in Jewish history.

The complete population of over 900 gathered together to be addressed by El'azar their commander. According to the account given by the contemporary historian Josephus Flavius, in his *Jewish War*, El'azar's speech so motivated the community that they all committed suicide, rather than be taken by the Romans. Here are two extracts from his stirring funeral oration:

*Let our wives die unabused, our children without knowledge of slavery: after that, let us do each other an ungrudging kindness, preserving our freedom as a glorious winding-sheet.*

*Come! while our hands are free and can hold a sword, let them do a noble service! Let us die unenslaved by our enemies, and leave this world as free men in company with our wives and children.*

The system of mass suicide was that each man went home to kill his wife and children; that done, ten men were chosen by lot to kill the remaining male population; one man was then chosen from the ten to kill the other nine; the one remaining man then fell on his own sword. The next day, when the Romans finally breached the wall from their ramp, they found all personal possessions burned, and their owners dead in their homes. Even hardened Roman campaigners must have been struck dumb by the death and destruction they met. The Zealots were careful to leave their plentiful supplies of food in evidence, to show the victors they were not being starved into submission. Josephus recorded that five children and two women, hiding in an underground cistern, did not die and lived to tell this grisly tale. 'Masada shall not fall again' is now the Israeli slogan, fashioned out of the Zealots' self-sacrifice at Masada.

Because Masada remained undiscovered for so many centuries, its excavation unearthed a wealth of information about the people who lived there and their way of life. For example there are the remains of a small synagogue, probably the oldest in existence and contemporary with the Temple in Jerusalem. I expressed surprise at the small size of this building, but Andrew pointed out that only a few Zealots would have attended their synagogue. To be a Zealot didn't mean you had to spend hours every day at worship. Herod certainly wasn't a familiar figure there. Don't miss Herod's bathhouse: a very sophisticated system including a *frigidarium*, a *tepidarium* and a *calidarium* (cold, hot and hotter)! In the hot room you can see the stone pillars, originally between two floors; steamy hot air passed from the stove below, through earthenware pipes, to create a Turkish-bath effect. The modern sauna employs exactly the same principle: water thrown on a hot stove to give off the required steam. There are frescoes to be seen which

Herod himself commissioned and perhaps admired. There's a tanner's workshop, storerooms and endless cisterns for catching the water.

Because it means so much to Israel, Masada is a well-kept, well-organized monument. Small booklets are available at the entrance for a shekel or two, and once inside, most places are well marked with posters and signs. You can walk up the Snake Path if you're feeling energetic, and you have 40 minutes to spare; but most people prefer the cable-car, which gives a spectacular view over the Dead Sea as you ascend and descend in a matter of minutes. Once out of the cable-car on the top, you still have some steps to climb. There are restaurants, souvenir shops and a car park at the base of the mountain.

## *En Gedi*

Excitement rose as we left Masada and approached En Gedi, the place where you can have your dip in the Dead Sea. Don't forget your swimming things. We enjoyed a self-service lunch at the restaurant, changed in the rather basic locker-rooms and emerged to try our luck in the sea where you float whether you want to or not. It's a strange experience, trying to swim in water which seems to resist your every effort. Breast-stroke or crawl is impossible; somehow your legs won't lie down, they insist on bobbing up all the time behind you. The most successful stroke is on your back, where you simply lie there and let the density of the salt water take the strain. It's true—you float like a cork! The feel of the water is curious; somehow salty and oily at the same time. And be careful not to let it get into your eyes—it stings like mad. Fortunately there are showers on the pebbly beach which you'll most certainly welcome to wash off the heavy salt deposit you've been immersed in. It's an experience not to be missed.

The Dead Sea is so salty largely because there is no outflow of water; when it flows in from the river Jordan at the sea's northern tip, it stays there. It's also the lowest place in the world, with temperatures that reach 130° F in the summer months and don't vary all that much in winter time. That intense heat causes an immense amount of evaporation to take place. Add to that the minerals (including bitumen) being drawn off the surface for commercial reasons—leaving behind a very salty, oily concoction. You can even observe at the edge of the sea weeds and rushes that at first look as though they're covered in frost or light snow. It's actually a crusty covering of solid salt. The level of the Dead Sea is getting steadily lower as each year goes by, because water is being drawn off the river further upstream for more and more irrigation. The net result is a parting of the sea half-way along its length, in effect making two large pools. This is evident looking from Masada over the sea towards the east.

## Qumran

From En Gedi we retraced our steps back along the western edge of the Dead Sea to Qumran, famous for the Dead Sea scrolls. The way these scrolls were found is a classic biblical story in itself. A bedouin boy was out looking after his herd of goats, when one of them wandered off into a cave. To frighten it out again, he threw a stone after it, which hit an earthenware jar inside the cave. The lad examined the jar and found it to contain what looked like old rags. Wrapped in these cloths were manuscripts. These documents, many well preserved, had lain hidden for almost 2,000 years. More jars were found containing scrolls, and the bedouin took them off to Bethlehem to a cobbler called Kando who they knew had an interest in antiquities. He realized they were ancient manuscripts, and together with the American Schools of Oriental Research, he began a systematic collection of all the scrolls which could be found. Only after the scrolls were discovered, was it realized that this site at Qumran was where the scrolls had originated. As far as is known, they were written by a community of the sect known as the Essenes who wrote two main types of scrolls: first, copies of the Old Testament which are a thousand years older than the Masoretic texts which, until this discovery, were commonly used as the main source for translation from the Hebrew. Here was an opportunity to compare one with the other. Nowadays, all modern versions of the Bible since the Dead Sea scrolls discovery incorporate whatever new light the scrolls have cast. The scrolls didn't teach anything new; they served more as a confirmation of what was already known from other sources. The Essenes, a small orthodox Jewish sect, organized on monastic lines, also wrote documents for use in their own religious community: for example, *The Manual of Discipline*, which enshrined their rule of life. So strict was their orthodoxy, they believed all other Jews had strayed from the true path of righteousness. They called themselves the 'sons of light', everyone else 'sons of darkness'. It's said their religious enthusiasm even forbade visits to the lavatory on the Sabbath!

The ruins of the Essene community buildings are there to be seen, on the banks of the Dead Sea. You can see the ritual bathing area, and the scriptorium where the transcribing took place. Fascinatingly enough, benches, writing desks and ink wells (still containing traces of carbon pigment) were found during the excavations. This is the actual room, where scribes took dictation as they wrote. The main meeting hall has also been identified. The idea that St John the Baptist was an Essene, or a member of a similar community, isn't beyond the bounds of possibility. If he wasn't a member, he certainly would have known about them as he wandered in the wilderness. The Essenes felt called into the same wilderness to preserve their pure religious way of life, which they felt they couldn't do in Jerusalem. They considered the Temple worship and the rule of King Herod corrupt. These were the desert fathers bridging the period between the old covenant and the time of Christ.

The demise of the Essene settlement came during the Roman crackdown in AD 70. Those who escaped, after hiding their scrolls in nearby caves, probably went down to Masada, joined the Zealots there, and met their end with them on the great rock. The ruins here really are ruins: everything is at ground or lower than ground level. You have to rely on a good guide or a book, and the signs directing you from one area to another.

The scrolls were discovered in 1947 and then dispersed throughout the academic world for translation. Andrew lamented the fact that a good 50 per cent of the scrolls have not yet been published. They are mostly in the United States, being sat upon while an anxious world has to wait until those who have them decide to publish them. David told us how he came to this area hundreds of times during the war and never once thought of looking in the caves!

If you want to see some of the scrolls, many are housed in the Shrine of the Book, attached to the Israel Museum in Jerusalem, near the Knesset (Parliament). There you can see the parchment roller which is the complete book of Isaiah. It's quite legible and comprises several pieces of skin sewn together.

Day two was now coming to an end. We boarded the bus and, as darkness began to descend, made our way back to Jerusalem. On the way I sat next to David who, at my invitation, briefly told me his life story, some details of which I have already mentioned. We arrived back quite tired at the Notre Dame Centre around 6.30. The pace of a ten-day tour of the Holy Land was beginning to tell.

# DAY 3

# Dominus Flevit, Gethsemane and the real Way of the Cross

A group of Roman Catholic American priests were staying at the Notre Dame Centre—a favourite watering hole for clerics, who qualify for a healthy discount. I arranged to see a couple of them in the foyer after supper late in the evening. One was a young man, born in Northern Ireland, who had emigrated to the States in the 1960s and was now a priest in the archdiocese of Los Angeles. This was his first time in Israel. What did he make of it?

'It strikes me as a place with tremendous historical hurts and pain, and there's a great deal of sadness in the city, and in people's lives too. The holy places have shown us not only that there's a lot of division between Muslim and Jew, but also there's division between Christian and Christian, and we have to work and heal in those places. The whole experience has been very moving and it's given me a complete new awareness of the life Jesus lived, and also I've become better informed of the political situation of this region and what a delicate and difficult thing it is to work out.

'In my childhood I always thought these places had a charm and a mystique about them; some of the places are quite ordinary, some beautiful and grand, and other places haven't touched me at all. That doesn't mean to say I'm deflated in any way. Now I've seen it and it's become a reality for me. A lot of the places are not glorious—but Jerusalem's history hasn't always been glorious either.'

The other priest was born in California of Mexican immigrant parents. It was also his first visit to the Holy Land.

'My greatest impression is the mixture of people from so

many different backgrounds and the scale of the conflict which exists here. My impression of that conflict has changed considerably since I came here. In the US we have tremendous support for the state of Israel, which is a good thing for the interests of the United States. But for the good of the world? Then my impressions are beginning to change. Mainly because I have now seen the Palestinians in a different light.

'The holy places have made my faith come alive, and for my own ministry things are now going to change. My preaching will be different; my study of the scriptures will be different; and my evaluation of world events will definitely change. Perhaps what impressed us all as a group was the church of Dominus Flevit, looking over the whole city of Jerusalem, and experiencing a certain amount of sadness, and thinking to ourselves how our Lord must have seen what would happen to the holy city. And I wish I could change all the conflict in the city which is there today—not all that much different from the city in Jesus' time.'

The Northern Irish-born priest was also impressed with the church where Jesus wept.

'The idea of Jesus weeping here really did touch me. Here was a city torn apart by divisions—not unlike where I come from in Northern Ireland. It made a lot of us weep inside, and that nothing short of divine intervention is going to solve this problem. Another place which touched me was the Wailing Wall; watching those people worship with such reverence. And then going up to the Dome of the Rock and watching Muslims worship with great reverence. Both communities treating us very lovingly but yet tearing each other apart. I met an Eastern Orthodox priest who told me 'this is your home too', which was very charming. But you can't wander around here and not be aware of the tension and the conflict that is going on all around. So, at the very least, this has been a very enlightening experience.'

## Dominus Flevit

It was a coincidence, after talking to the two American priests about Dominus Flevit, that our first stop on the third day was the church of Dominus Flevit ('the Lord wept'), to the east of the city. The site was not marked by a church until Crusader times. It fell into ruins and wasn't rebuilt until the Franciscans excavated the plot and built the church early this century. In the process of excavations, little ossuaries were found—small boxes containing the bones of the dead. Each of the boxes had a motif on the side—a rosette, or a palm tree—and some were found to bear the sign of the cross, proof that in the early centuries there were Judaeo-Christians in Jerusalem. On 50 of these boxes were found names familiar to us from the Bible, common Jewish everyday names such as Mary, Martha, Matthew, Joseph and Jesus. Most of these bone boxes can be seen at the Franciscan friary by the church of the Flagellation on the Via Dolorosa, but a number can be seen at Dominus Flevit.

The church was built by the Italian architect Barluzzi in the mid-1950s. The main altar does not face east as is usual, but west in this case. If you stand at the back of the church, and look out over the Kidron valley towards the Dome of the Rock, you can see how the cross on the altar lines up directly with the Dome built on the site of the Temple Jesus knew. When we arrived at the church, it had been taken over by a large group of Germans who were hearing Mass. Andrew decided to have the readings outside, in the rather pleasant church grounds with flowers and plants and birds singing in the trees.

LUKE 13:34–35

Jerusalem, Jerusalem, you that kill the prophets and stone those that are sent to you! How often have I longed to gather your children together, as a hen gathers her brood under her wings, and you refused! Look! Your house will be left to you. Yes, I promise you, you shall not see me till the time comes when you are saying: Blessed is he who is coming in the name of the Lord.

LUKE 19:41–44

As he drew near and came in sight of the city he shed tears over it and said, 'If you too had only recognized on this day the way to peace! But in fact it is hidden from your eyes! Yes, a time is coming when your enemies will raise fortifications all around you, when they will encircle you and hem you in on every side; they will dash you and your children inside your walls to the ground; they will leave not one stone standing on another within you, because you did not recognize the moment of your visitation.'

But why specifically did Jesus weep over the city at this spot? Largely because his people were oppressed people and also he felt God was being ignored because Temple worship was not in keeping with what it should have been. One wonders would Jesus weep all over again if he came back and looked over Jerusalem again? He probably would: the oppression, the division between two nations—he'd weep just the same. Only the names are different 2,000 years on.

*You drew near to the city, Lord,*
*and wept over it.*
*Here in this beautiful garden*
*and in this simple church*
*with its altar overlooking the holy city*
*we could weep with you*
*over your city.*

*'Would that even today you knew the things*
*that make for peace.*
*But now they are hid from your eyes.'*
*These words are as true today*
*as when you first spoke them here.*
*We pray for the peace of Jerusalem,*
*once dashed to the ground*
*because she did not know the time of her visitation.*

*We join our prayers with you, Lord,*
*for the peace of this holy city*

*which is so dear to our hearts
as it was to yours.*

Jesus would have been with his disciples when he came here and wept. They were actually on their way down the slope to the foot of the Kidron valley, to the garden of Gethsemane. It was a quiet spot outside the noisy city. His arrival on the Mount of Olives at Dominus Flevit (probably not the exact spot, but nearby) is really the beginning of Jesus' Passion. It was approaching the feast of the Passover, and excitement was building in Jerusalem in preparation for the event. But did Jesus know what was in store for him, and that within days he would be hanging on the cross? Very likely he did. Not long before, he had said to his disciples that he was going to go to Jerusalem and the Son of man must die. Then he set his face steadfastly towards Jerusalem; and from that point on he knew his destiny. My mind then jumped straight to the big question: Did Jesus at any time during his life know that he was the Christ, the Messiah? He probably had within him a growing realization, supported by a strong inclination from his baptism by John. Then, during the temptation in the wilderness, he wrestled and battled with himself to know his real identity. At Caesarea Philippi Peter confessed that Jesus was the Christ, the son of the blessed, and Jesus began to prophesy that soon he would experience suffering and death. Along with that realization there was also a growing fear, plainly illustrated in the garden of Gethsemane when he asked for the cup of suffering to be taken from him. Our inclination is to think Jesus simply accepted this sequence of events with equanimity. What is often forgotten is that he was a human being, and must have been very frightened at the prospect.

### Garden of Gethsemane *(Garden of the Olive Press)*

We walked downhill for some ten minutes; we negotiated ourselves successfully through a persistent crowd of street vendors offering the usual postcards, jewellery and olive-wood statues, and came eventually to the Franciscan church of All Nations. In the garden of the church are eight very ancient olive trees. Some guides claim these were here in the time of Jesus; whereas in reality they are hundreds rather than thousands of years old. There is an old saying among Jews that an olive tree never dies; it always sends out shoots from which the new tree grows. So perhaps the gnarled old olives here are literally offshoots of those Jesus and his disciples knew.

In Jesus' time the whole of this side of the Mount of Olives was covered with olive trees; and at the foot of the mount there would have been an olive press, similar to the one we'd seen at Bethany the day before. This site (or certainly one near to here) was a favourite meeting place for Jesus and his disciples; it was outside the city, away from the crowds, where they could talk, meditate and pray. It's hard to imagine that scene today as the traffic on the nearby main road roars by. It was here that Jesus spent the night of the agony before his arrest, after the Last Supper. Here, Jesus prayed to decide what to do: either to face certain arrest or make his escape over the Mount of Olives and back to his friends in Bethany. As he prayed his lonely vigil, the disciples fell asleep several times, even though Jesus expressed his disappointment that they could not even 'watch one hour'. Being one of the disciples, Judas would have known this spot, and as dawn broke soldiers, led by Judas, arrested Jesus and took him to the house of Caiaphas.

LUKE 22:39–48, 54
He then left to make his way as usual to the Mount of Olives, with the disciples following. When he reached the place he said to them, 'Pray not to be put to the test.'
  Then he withdrew from them, about a stone's throw away, and knelt down and prayed. 'Father,' he said, 'if you are willing, take this cup away from me. Nevertheless, let your will be done, not mine.' Then an angel appeared to him, coming from heaven to give him strength. In his anguish he prayed even more earnestly, and his sweat fell to the ground like great drops of blood.

When he rose from prayer he went to his disciples and found them sleeping for sheer grief. And he said to them, 'Why are you asleep? Get up and pray not to be put to the test.' Suddenly, while he was still speaking, a number of men appeared, and at the head of them the man called Judas, one of the Twelve, who went up to Jesus to kiss him. Jesus said, 'Judas, are you betraying the son of man with a kiss?' ... They seized him and led him away, and they took him to the high priest's house.

## *The Church of All Nations*

This Franciscan church was built from contributions donated by Roman Catholics throughout the world, hence this popular name. Inside you'll see that all contributing nations have their coat of arms set into the wall. Its other name is the basilica of the Agony, and just before the high altar there's an outcrop of rock: traditionally the place where Jesus sweated his blood the night before he was arrested.

The first church on this site was built in the fourth century. When that was razed to the ground during the Persian invasion, the site remained undeveloped until the arrival of the Crusaders in the twelfth century. Their church remained for almost 200 years and then fell into disuse. The Franciscans regained possession of the site in the sixteenth century, but the present church wasn't built until 1924. It is very gloomy inside; what light there is comes through rather striking modern stained glass windows. (If you want to take photos of some of the splendid mosaics a powerful flash is necessary.) It's a place where the silence that is requested helps preserve an atmosphere of prayerfulness.

We left the church and had another look at the well-kept garden, with benches to sit on and plenty of greenery to look at, and as usual the purple and white bougainvillaea tumbling over the hedges. But I could still hear the considerable noise of the traffic on the main road which runs across the front of the garden and the church. However, not everyone felt as I did. Several of the party were very moved by what they saw, and felt very strongly the associations of Jesus' sufferings on this spot.

From the front of the church (or across the road for an even better view) you can see three Jewish tombs at the very bottom of the Kidron valley: the tomb of Absalom, the pillar of Zachariah, and the cave tomb of St James. These three tombs date from the first century BC and therefore were in place during the lifetime of Jesus. As he walked down from Jerusalem out to Bethany, or to Gethsemane, he would have seen those tombs and recognized them as familiar landmarks. What we were looking at, Jesus also would have looked at. There's not an awful lot about which you can say that with such a fair degree of certainty. We stopped here for a while to pray, and Andrew read from his own book.

Agony
and bloody sweat.
That is what Gethsemane is all about.
This beautiful garden
was once a favourite meeting-place
for you and your disciples, Lord.
Yet here the Shepherd was struck
and the sheep of the flock were scattered.

'Father, if it is your will,
let this cup pass from me.'
But no, Lord.
You had to drink that cup
right down to the dregs
to the very last drop.
Help us to do your Father's will
until it hurts
and on through the agony.

We are with you now, Lord,
in the place of your Agony
where your sweat fell like drops of blood

upon the rock—this rock?
Help us as we watch with you
the agonies and sufferings of the world
and see you there.


**Almighty Father,**
look with mercy on this your family
for which our Lord Jesus Christ
   was content to be betrayed
   and given up into the hands of wicked men
   and to suffer death upon the cross;
who is alive and glorified
with you and the Holy Spirit,
one God, now and for ever.

*Pray Every Day*

## Tomb of the Virgin

Nearby to the church of All Nations is an underground cave reputed to be where the Virgin Mary, the mother of Jesus, is buried. This is a jewel of a place, not to be missed. There is, however, a conflicting story about where Mary is actually buried. When Jesus died on the cross he committed his mother to the care of John, the beloved disciple. As far as we know, John, together with Mary, went to Ephesus, in present-day Turkey, to live and to teach. John spent his final years there, and presumably so did Mary. Thus, though the Jerusalem tradition has it that Mary is buried near to the church of All Nations, the New Testament reference supports Mary's move to Ephesus. This shrine is mainly administered by the Armenian, Greek Orthodox and Ethiopian Churches. We edged our way down a long flight of stone steps into the darkness. The smell of incense was still hanging in the air from an early morning liturgy. The tomb itself is in solid rock, isolated in the middle of the church and is similar in style to Christ's tomb in the church of the Holy Sepulchre.

### St Peter in Gallicantu

We jumped into our bus again and drove to the south side of the Old City to the head of the Kidron valley. Again a crowd of sellers blocked our path, but by now we were all adept at side-stepping the eager vendors who offered the usual merchandise, plus Arab headdresses. However, it must be admitted that on our departure from St Peter's, those of us who couldn't resist the blandishments of the most persistent hawkers, climbed back aboard the bus trying to look like Lawrence of Arabia!

The foundations underneath this church are thought to have been the courtyard of the house of Caiaphas where Jesus was taken after being arrested in the garden of Gethsemane. If you remember, Peter was the only disciple to follow Jesus and the soldiers when they arrested him. Once at the house, Peter (to his credit) at least stayed around to await the outcome of the arrest. Several servants at the house recognized Peter as one of Jesus' followers. Peter hotly denied this charge three times.

MARK 14:66–72

While Peter was down below in the courtyard, one of the high priest's servant-girls came up. She saw Peter warming himself there, looked closely at him and said, 'You too were with Jesus, the man from Nazareth.' But he denied it. 'I do not know, I do not understand what you are talking about,' he said. And he went out into the forecourt, and a cock crowed. The servant-girl saw him again and started telling the bystanders, 'This man is one of them.' But again he denied it. A little later the bystanders themselves said to Peter, 'You are certainly one of them! Why, you are a Galilean.' But he started cursing and swearing, 'I do not know the man you speak of.' And at once the cock crowed for the second time, and Peter recalled what Jesus had said to him, 'Before the cock crows twice, you will have disowned me three times.' And he burst into tears.

We then descended to a lower level, and Andrew clarified

for us how the Jews scourged their prisoners. The hapless victim—and this may well have happened to Jesus—was firmly lashed between two stone pillars, spread-eagled and given 'forty lashes save one'. The thorns that Jesus was crowned with, from local thorn trees, would have been set into the ends of the whip with which he was, by tradition, scourged. Look for the holes in the floor where salt, water and hyssop were kept. If the prisoner survived this punishment (and many did not) these solutions were applied to the wounds to keep them clean. This gave us all a graphic example of what the torture Jesus experienced was like, though it's uncertain whether Jesus was actually scourged. On the other hand, St Paul in his epistles, does mention that he received the 'forty stripes save one' on three occasions. There's even a window here, through which a guard would have kept his eye on prisoners both in this dungeon, and also those in another dungeon on a lower level. He would lean through the window with his foot on a special mark, still there to be seen, and his elbow on the sill of the window or opening.

## David's Tomb

Extending beyond the Zion Gate, forming the most southerly outcrop of the Old City, is Mount Zion where we saw the tomb of David. Curiously, it seems that this is definitely not the place where King David was laid to rest. More likely it was on the south-eastern hill below where the Temple was and not here in the south-west.

1 KINGS 2:10

So David fell asleep with his ancestors and was buried in the City of David. David was king of Israel for a period of forty years: he reigned at Hebron for seven years, and in Jerusalem for thirty-three.

The tomb is obviously a Jewish shrine, and after the Western

Wall, the holiest of places for Jews. The actual spot which is venerated as being David's tomb, the cenotaph, is decorated with many Jewish symbols: the scroll, the star (five points for Solomon, six points for David, as on the Israeli flag), the menorah, the crown symbolizing kingship, and the letters in Hebrew which read 'David, king of Israel'. Across one of the courtyards is an exhibition displaying mementos of those who died in the Holocaust.

## *St Stephen's (or Lion's) Gate*

We retraced our steps along the eastern side of the Old City up as far as St Stephen's Gate. Here it was that Stephen, a Greek-speaking Jew, 'full of faith and power', one of the first deacons to be appointed by the apostles, the first martyr, was stoned to death. He probably cared for the Greek-speaking Christian community in Jerusalem at the time. He was denounced to the Jewish council as a blasphemer, taken outside the gate and put to death.

We then walked up into the Old City towards St Anne's church and the Pool of Bethesda. It was quiet as we made our way up the narrow street because the Palestinians had called for a lightning one-day strike. This is all part of the *intifada* (the uprising). However, had that not happened the streets would have been filled with the hustle and the bustle of people buying and selling, going from place to place; very much as it would have been in Jesus' time. The church of St Anne, said to be one of the finest Crusader buildings in the whole of the city, was built on Byzantine foundations and occupied for some time by a congregation of nuns. The crypt is said to be the site of the home of Mary's parents, Anne and Joachim. The church is now in the care of the White Fathers. The acoustics are so impressive that, like many pilgrims visiting this church, we all burst into song. But as usual none of us knew enough words of any one hymn to allow any sort of creditable impromptu performance. However, we tried; and for a few short moments the church did ring to the much enhanced notes of our tiny group.

We emerged from St Anne's around midday—the time for Muslim prayer. From many minarets the muezzins called the faithful to their worship; their wailings clashing and rolling with each other between the sunlit sky and the city rooftops. Accompanied by this not unpleasant sound, we walked a little way from St Anne's to the Pool of Bethesda (which is all in the same complex). The pool was dug around 200 BC as a reservoir to collect water for the Temple. It also became a place of healing, and perhaps it was here that Jesus healed the paralytic.

JOHN 5:1–9

After this there was a Jewish festival, and Jesus went up to Jerusalem. Now in Jerusalem next to the Sheep Pool, there is a pool called Bethesda in Hebrew, which has five porticos; and under these were crowds, blind, lame, paralysed. One man there had an illness which had lasted thirty-eight years, and when Jesus saw him lying there and knew that he had been in that condition for a long time, he said 'Do you want to be well again?' 'Sir,' replied the sick man, 'I have no one to put me into the pool when the water is disturbed; and while I am still on the way, someone else gets down there before me.' Jesus said, 'Get up, pick up your sleeping-mat and walk around.' The man was cured at once, and he picked up his mat and started to walk around.

The Jews objected to Jesus' healing the paralytic on the Sabbath, and also to his calling God his Father. In the church you can see a fragment of a mosaic floor belonging to the Byzantine church built over the site, and also the remains of the apse of the later Crusader church built over the water's source, the spring itself.

The nearest we came to any disturbances was here at Bethesda, when suddenly stones were lobbed over a high wall opposite to where we were standing. The stones were big enough, but we suspected the throwers were just little lads making sure we didn't forget they were there.

## Via Dolorosa *(Way of Sorrows)*

For any pilgrim to the Holy Land this must be one of the most poignant moments of the entire visit. Certainly during this long walk of agony, the innocent man, already tortured, beaten and humiliated, must have known his end was near. From the moment he entered the city for the feast of Passover: weeping over the city, eating with his disciples, the agony in the garden, the arrest, the trial by Pilate at the Citadel, the scourging and crowning with thorns, and finally the burden of the great cross on his back—all these momentous events had led him to this Way of Sorrows. It's most likely in the light of the most recent archaeological evidence and historical interpretation that the real Way of the Cross, the one Jesus trod, actually began at the Citadel, just inside and south of the Jaffa Gate on the west side of the city. If this was Pilate's house, then the trial would have taken place there. It's likely that Jesus would have set out from there wearing the crown of thorns and carrying the cross. The route was then in a direction due north to Golgotha, the hill where criminals were executed and actually only a few hundred yards from the Citadel. You can walk it in a few minutes. In those days, of course, Golgotha was outside the city walls before the boundaries were changed to their present-day positions.

The more historically accurate route is the one marked by dots on the map, p.x), according to Fr Richard M. Mackowski's book *Jerusalem: City of Jesus* (Wm. B. Eerdmans, 1980).

> The trial took place in the public square of the upper city, which we identify with the compound of the Armenian Orthodox Patriarchate, very probably close to the cathedral of St James. Pilate's Praetorium, formerly of the palace of Herod the Great, has been established archaeologically as built on the property where the Armenian Orthodox Seminary now stands. The barracks and the courtyard of the procurator's praetorium guard we identify with

the present Citadel and Kishleh compound, the Israeli police post inside the Old City walls [see map] ... Here Pilate ordered the Roman soldiers to scourge Jesus before he finally sentenced him to death. The speaker's platform on which was placed Pilate's judgment seat would also have been located in the present compound of St James' Cathedral of the Armenian Orthodox Church. This would also be where Jesus and the two other condemned criminals received their crossbeams, and here began the sorrowful way of the cross through the streets of Jerusalem. It was the custom to parade the condemned criminals in order to teach others a lesson. This route, according to our interpretation, can also be traced in the streets of the Armenian Quarter today: St James' Street (or the Street of the Armenians) veering eastwards as far as the junction of Suq el-Hussor, the former Cardo Maximus of the Emperor Hadrian's Aelia Capitolina, then turning at a right angle northwards towards the ancient Garden Gate, preserved at the junction where the four principal streets of the Old City meet: David Street from the west, Chain Street from the east, Suq el-Attarin (the southern portion of the Suq Khan ez-Zeit leading southwards from the Damascus Gate) and the Suq el-Hussor from the south. The Good Friday procession would then have continued northwards up to a certain point where it veered in a north-westerly direction towards Golgotha.

However, since the sixteenth century most of the fourteen stations of the cross (plaques marking the main events leading up to the Crucifixion) have been spaced along another route. (The final stations are in the church of the Holy Sepulchre.) This is a form of devotion which grew up in Europe, and when it was transferred to Jerusalem it had to fit the geographical location. So, the traditional Way of the Cross, conducted by the Franciscan friars every Friday starting at 3.00 p.m., is a longer route enabling crowds of pilgrims to follow in procession; but it isn't the authentic route which Jesus was obliged to follow. For most pilgrims, however, such geographical niceties are quite irrelevant in a city steeped in memories and devotion. The first station (Jesus is condemned to death) starts in the courtyard of the Muslim school—opposite the Ecce Homo church of the Sisters of Sion which has been built on the site where the Antonia Fortress used to be. Herod built this fortress some 40 years before Christ and named it after Mark Antony. From this garrison soldiers could look over the Temple area and anticipate trouble should it threaten to break out.

On the Friday afternoon I joined the friars, and hundreds of others, and we followed the fourteen stations of Jesus by a circuitous route through the narrow streets. This particular devotion is popular with Roman Catholics, especially during the season of Lent. Here in Jerusalem, I found it a rather business-like affair with the lead friar chanting and praying through a hand-held megaphone. He travelled from one station to another with great speed and little apparent devotion. A rather solemn-faced Muslim gentleman in a red fez cleared the way with a parade-ground baton if the crowds pressed too tightly on the friars as they walked with amazing speed from one commemorative wall-plaque to another. We finished in the church of the Holy Sepulchre. The crowds on Calvary were so numerous it was pointless even trying to climb the stone stairway. The final station was before the tomb itself: the promise of Resurrection after the Crucifixion. An interesting experience, but don't expect a lot of devotion.

### *Ecce Homo* (*Behold the man*)

This is one church not to be missed. The sanctuary is quite stunning in the way a remnant of the Old City has been used to fashion a modern place of Christian worship. A triumphal arch was erected here by Hadrian to celebrate the end of the Second Jewish Revolt in AD 135. It was a three-bay arch, and thankfully one of those arches survives as the reredos of Ecce Homo church. The conversion is tasteful, and magnetic in its appeal. We stood for a long time admiring it. Archaeologically speaking, the basement of the church holds even more wonders. There is a magnificent pavement—complete with ridges to help chariot wheels grip in the wet—once thought to have been the place where Pilate said 'Behold the Man' as he presented Jesus to the crowd (John 19:5). In spite of Pilate's finding him innocent, the crowd insisted that Jesus should die. As it is now more probable that this trial happened at the Citadel, the nuns have ceased calling the pavement Gabbatha—the 'pavement' of John 19:13—now it's known simply as one of the main thoroughfares of old Jerusalem. This pavement, put there by Hadrian about a hundred years after Christ, leads across to the church of the Flagellation which commemorates Jesus' scourging before he began his way to the cross. In honour of tradition rather than archaeological fact, we stopped for two readings here.

JOHN 19:2–6

Pilate then had Jesus taken away and scourged; and after this, the soldiers twisted some thorns into a crown and put it on his head and dressed him in a purple robe. They kept coming up to him and saying, 'Hail, king of the Jews!' and slapping him in the face.

Pilate came outside again and said to them, 'Look, I am going to bring him out to let you see that I find no case against him.' Jesus then came out wearing the crown of thorns and the purple robe. Pilate said, 'Here is the man.' When they saw him, the chief priests and the guards shouted, 'Crucify him! Crucify him!'

MARK 15:1–6

First thing in the morning, the chief priests, together with the elders and the scribes, and the rest of the Sanhedrin, had their plan ready. They had Jesus bound and took him away and handed him over to Pilate.

Pilate put to him this question, 'Are you the king of the Jews?' He replied, 'It is you who say it.' And the chief priests brought many accusations against him. Pilate questioned him again, 'Have you no reply at all? See how many accusations they are bringing against you!' But, to Pilate's surprise, Jesus made no further reply.

*A pavement.*
*Keep on the pavement, Lord.*

It is the sure way to get you there:
to the cross.

Pilate tried to release you,
but it was not to be;
the chief priests saw to that.
So Pilate brought you out
and sat down on the judgement seat
at a place called Gabbatha—
the pavement—here.

Here Pilate handed you over, Lord,
to be crucified. And you went out,
bearing your own cross.
But not before the soldiers
had had their way with you.
Mock homage.
You were beaten,
spat upon,
and mocked.
And yet you kept to the pavement, Lord.
You knew the way you had to go
to fulfil your Father's will.

Keep me to the pavement, Lord:
the narrow way that I must tread
if I am to follow you.

O God, the Father of mankind, who didst suffer thine only Son to be set forth as a spectacle despised, derided, and scornfully arrayed, yet in his humiliation to reveal his majesty: Draw us, we beseech thee, both to behold the man and to worship the king, immortal, eternal, world without end.
*Daily Prayer*

The reading from the gospels, together with Andrew's own

commentary, prompted a question: If Jesus was innocent as charged, why didn't he say so at his trial before Pilate? Jesus probably realized at this point that the only way he could accomplish the will of God was to remain silent; to have entered into a wrangle with either the religious or the Roman leaders would not have done anything to advance the kingdom of God. From the night of the agony in Gethsemane, he accepted that a chain of events was to lead to Calvary and the cross.

On my first trip to Jerusalem for the BBC in 1982, Fr Jerome Murphy-O'Connor showed me the authentic Way of the Cross, which took us a matter of minutes to complete. Starting at the Citadel just inside the Jaffa Gate on the west side of the city, we walked down into the narrow streets and alleyways of the suq, occasionally glimpsing the open sky, but more often than not threading our way through dark and cavernous tunnels choked with people and merchandise, the odd donkey and playing children. Near to the church of the Holy Sepulchre we came to a wider, open street with broad, tiered steps to accommodate the gradual slope. According to Fr Murphy-O'Connor, Jesus would have stumbled his way along this route, bearing the cross. Jesus' burden was a heavy, straight beam of wood strapped across his shoulders. This was the cross-piece that slotted across the top of a fixed upright piece of wood that was already in place as a permanent fixture on Calvary. As Jesus walked, he had to negotiate the wide steps, and if he stumbled, with his hands and arms lashed to the beam across his back, he would be unable to protect himself as he fell. Consequently the whole of the front of his body, including his face, would smash against the ground as he went down under the weight of the beam. As we slowly retraced these steps, the stalls were open, people were buying and selling, hawkers were shouting their wares and the donkeys brayed and made a mess. Overhead, carpets and bolts of cloth were on display creating welcome shade from the burning heat. The whole prospect was not so different from the time of Jesus. Here was just another common criminal being taken to the place of execution accompanied by a few soldiers who held up a placard saying who he was and why he was going to die. Two thieves were also on their way to die. There was no need to shut the shop, or indeed take any notice: business as usual. Shortly we made a left turn—and there was the church of the Holy Sepulchre. In the time of Jesus, Golgotha (Calvary in Latin), the place where executions took place, was outside the city walls near a rubbish dump. Over the centuries the city has changed and expanded its boundaries, so now the church of the Holy Sepulchre and Golgotha are within the walls. After the sacking of Jerusalem in AD 70 this whole area was a rubbish dump. Emperor Constantine (274–338) built the original basilica (prompted by his mother Helena who by tradition found the True Cross here) and incorporated into it both Calvary and the tomb.

LUKE 23:39–43

One of the criminals hanging there abused him: 'Are you not the Christ? Save yourself and us as well.' But the other spoke up and rebuked him. 'Have you no fear of God at all?' he said. 'You got the same sentence as he did, but in our case we deserved it: we are paying for what we did. But this man has done nothing wrong.' Then he said, 'Jesus, remember me when you come into your kingdom.' He answered him, 'In truth, I tell you, today you will be with me in paradise.'

## Church of the Holy Sepulchre

The present church dates from Crusader times, and is built on a much less grand scale than Constantine's original. Curiously, down the centuries this most holy of Christian shrines has been neglected. The whole crumbling shambles almost fell down completely during the British Mandate until some British Tommies shored it up with heavy scaffolding. Since then plans have been put forward to tear down and rebuild the whole complex, but so far these have been rejected. And the reason for that can be no great mystery: agreement for radical change would have to be approved by Latin Catholics, Greek Orthodox, Armenians, Copts, Syrians and Ethiopians. Nothing is simple when done by committee. However, once you become accustomed to being surrounded by heaps and heaps of unfinished business, the church has a certain magic, an attraction which needs time to begin to understand. There is, however, an attempt at the present time to restore the church to look more like it was in the time of Constantine. Inside you'll see a lot of rather unsightly restoration work. Above all there is the certainty that since the time of Constantine, this is where the whole Christian world has focused a good deal of its attention. The numbers who have come here to be at the place where Jesus was buried, and where he rose from the tomb, must count in tens of millions.

Passing from the courtyard, under the bell-tower and through the main entrance in the façade—all Crusader built—immediately in front of you is a large marble stone at ground level. This is the Stone of Anointing where, traditionally, the body of Jesus was prepared for burial. As we entered the church a Franciscan procession had just started and the air was filled with drifting Gregorian plainchant. We turned sharp right and climbed the stone staircase up to the summit of the rock of Calvary. We were confronted by two chapels: one belonging to the Latin Church, the other to the Greek Church. There are mosaics, icons with silver overlay, candles, hanging lamps and effigies of angels, the Virgin Mary, and other saintly figures. A figure of Christ crucified dominates the left-hand, Greek altar, flanked on either side by Our Lady and St John who followed him all the way. These altars on Calvary have probably looked much like this for some two or three hundred years.

Under the altar in the Greek chapel is a hole in the rock, said to be the spot where the cross was fixed. I, like many, crouched underneath the altar and placed my arm through the circular hole, and some eighteen inches down I touched a smooth, flat surface. For almost 2,000 years this place has been protected and revered by those who have believed Jesus died here. Archaeologists and historians also agree that this is the place where Jesus died on his cross. Despite the crowds, the complex building and the general disarray—and sometimes, to Western eyes, disrespect—some people are genuinely moved by their experience of being on the rock of Calvary. It's not unusual to see people in tears.

## The Tomb

We came down from Calvary and walked the 40 metres or so across the floor of the church to the tomb. Again, not what you'd expect; almost a small square church with a rather unattractive superstructure, within a huge domed church. At the rear of the tomb is the Coptic chapel, which is said to contain a tiny rock-cut remnant of the original tomb. The Victorian-looking edifice over the tomb was built in the early nineteenth century because of fire damage. The outside is festooned with hanging lamps, icons and candles, and inevitably there's a queue to get in. It's a one-way system: those coming out have to squeeze past those who are waiting to go in. As we stood in line, people in front were saying their rosary as the queue slowly shuffled forward. Eventually we entered the first chamber, the chapel of the Angels, which commemorates the disciples finding the angel sitting outside the tomb with the stone rolled away. Just to give some idea of the volume of people passing through this church; it opens at 4 a.m. and closes at 6.30 p.m. every day of the year, and there's always a queue.

We bent down low to enter the antechapel to the tomb, and then on into the chamber of the tomb. It's a very tiny room—about 6 feet by 5 feet—the length of the tomb itself. On the right is the tomb, now covered in marble. As at Calvary, there's little doubt that this *is* the tomb of Christ, and, like Calvary, it's certainly been regarded as such since the time of Constantine. A Greek Orthodox priest is often on duty within the rather stifling tomb chamber. One isn't encouraged to dwell for too long as others are pressing to get in. An icon of

View of Jerusalem from the Mount of Olives

Damascus Gate, Jerusalem

*Left:* Old City, Jerusalem
*Right:* Selling inside Damascus Gate

Wailing Wall and Dome of the Rock

Jews praying at the Wailing Wall

*Left:* Entrance to the Church of the Holy Sepulchre

*Below:* Armenian Chapel in the Church of the Holy Sepulchre. The only remnant of the original tomb is visible below the candle held by the monk.

*Left:* The courtyard of St George's Anglican Cathedral

*Right:* The courtyard at Acre

The synagogue at Capernaum

The caves of the Dead Sea Scrolls at Qumran

*Right:* Looking over the Sea of Galilee
*Below:* The Church of St Peter's Authority

The Via Dolorosa

View of Jerusalem from inside Church of Dominus Flevit

the risen Christ stands above the tomb on a marble shelf, surrounded by candles and flowers. While Western Christians emphasize this spot as the burial place of Jesus, Greek Orthodox (who have charge of it) tend to emphasize its more positive aspect; they call it the church of the Resurrection. As you come out of the tomb, just there in front is the Greek choir with its huge chandelier hanging above. Directly below the central point of the chandelier is, according to Greek Orthodox tradition, the centre of Christendom. Old maps of the world often depicted Jerusalem as the centre of the world—so here's the very kernel.

MATTHEW 28:1–7

After the Sabbath, and towards dawn on the first day of the week, Mary of Magdala and the other Mary went to visit the sepulchre. And suddenly there was a violent earthquake, for an angel of the Lord, descending from heaven, came and rolled the stone away and sat on it. His face was like lightning, his robe as white as snow. The guards were so shaken by fear of him that they were like dead men. But the angel spoke; and he said to the women, 'There is no need for you to be afraid. I know you are looking for Jesus, who was crucified. He is not here, for he has risen, as he said he would. Come and see the place where he lay, then go quickly and tell his disciples, "He has risen from the dead and now he is going ahead of you to Galilee; that is where you will see him."'

This had been by far our heaviest day, and as we walked back to Notre Dame the suq was more empty than is usual at this time of day—because of the general strike. Daylight soon goes in this part of the world; and before we knew it we were threading our way through the Old City in the dark. Feet were beginning to protest. We had a lot to talk about over dinner.

# DAY 4

## A meeting point of languages and faiths

On one of the free mornings I arranged to meet Canon Naim Ateek, one of the priests in charge of the Arabic-speaking Christian community at St George's Cathedral on the Nablus Road. We decided to sit in the garden which is over to the left of the cathedral through its hostel reception area. In this most unlikely setting of an English country garden—complete with wrought-iron garden furniture, English plants and flowers, surrounded by incessant birdsong which failed to drown out the noise of the traffic just over the high wall—Canon Ateek began by telling me how proud he and his family are of their Christianity, which they can trace back to the very first centuries. He emphasized this point at the very beginning of our conversation; he felt people automatically regard Christian Arabs as converts from Islam, whereas by the fourth century Palestine was a mainly Christian country, and Muhammad himself was not born until the sixth century.

Canon Ateek is from Galilee, the son of a very devout Orthodox Christian, a goldsmith by profession. As a boy, Naim attended both the local Anglican Church as well as the Orthodox. He feels he has had the best of both religious worlds. In 1948 the Israelis drove the family out of Galilee and they moved to Nazareth where they became members of the Anglican community. Naim always had the calling to be a priest, and when he was ordained he worked for five years in Haifa in the north before being appointed to the cathedral in Jerusalem. I remarked that we were sitting in what could very well be described as a little piece of England in a Middle Eastern setting. He was quick to agree. 'It is very interesting', he said with a huge smile, 'that many missionaries tried to implant a bit of their home country in the mission field; and I'm told this place resembles some places in and around the city of Oxford.'

I pointed out to Canon Ateek that over the centuries pilgrims like myself and the group I was with have come to the Holy Land and to Jerusalem to see all the places connected with early Christianity and the life of Jesus. For most visitors it's a once in a lifetime experience; and for many a memorable and a moving one. But I wondered, what effect did these holy places have on Palestinians like Naim and others who are born and brought up here? Does familiarity diminish the impact?

'There are two ways to express this', he replied, 'and the first is the way most of us feel about Palestine: we were born and brought up here and so it's our country. True, we do pass by these holy places every day, but we never forget that we are here in our *own* home. But there is the added religious significance, stemming from our religious faith and we feel privileged to have been born here. In a sense we fluctuate between these two sensations. But now because of the political situation I feel that people are more and more emphasizing not so much the historical sites as the "living stones". They are the Christians who live here; who are suffering and who are crying out for justice.'

I mentioned some of the inevitable observations we as a group were making, and the visible signs of unrest in and around Jerusalem: the soldiers, the guns, the searches, and the general security, which actually indicates insecurity. I also remarked on the tension in the city, which cannot be ignored, and the odd occasion when we had been prevented from keeping to our schedule because of the unrest between Arab and Jew.

'It's a constant agony for us, because I think our people want to live in peace. They want peace, but they are subjected to all kinds of torture, and all kinds of oppression. Life is not normal here and people feel that their political situation is deteriorating rapidly, in spite of a feeling that one day there will have to be a breakthrough in relations. There is a feeling of despair. Our treatment is becoming more and more brutal and oppressive: and that is taxing the people quite a lot. Jesus would probably have used the same words as he did when he stood on the Mount of Olives at Dominus Flevit, where he wept over the city 2,000 years ago. "As he drew near and came in sight of the city he shed tears over it and said, 'If you too had only recognized on this day the way to peace. But it is hidden from your eyes'" (Luke 19:41–43).

'One gets the feeling now that the leaders of the government of Israel do not really know what to do to bring about peace. Peace will come to this land not through oppression but as a result of understanding, negotiation and compromise. Because there is no way that the government of Israel can maintain control over all the land and oppress almost a million and a half Palestinians. This situation just cannot go on forever, and that isn't going to bring peace. That's why so many of us are literally crying at what is going on here. More people should be focusing on what will bring peace to this land and not concentrating on those policies which won't achieve that.

'You see, ever since 1967 people on the West Bank and Gaza have been living under occupation of the Israeli government and Israeli troops; and so, when we say people are living under occupation, this means they are living under military rule. They don't have any freedom and the military regime imposes its own rules and its own laws on the people: laws which are not perceived as being for the good of the people, but rather for the benefit of the occupier. These laws are oppressive laws, and that includes driving people from their homes, demolishing houses, deporting people, imposing curfews, closing schools and universities—all to keep people under control. Since 1987 and the *intifada* (the uprising) those laws have become harsher, and the people have resisted in largely non-violent ways. And what is most significant, in spite of our resolve, is that we Palestinians are not calling for an end to the Israeli state. But we are calling for an end to occupation. We want our own Palestinian state where we can live in freedom, dignity and democracy.'

As someone who gleaned most of his information from the media, it seemed to me that for as long as I and many others can remember there has been conflict between Arab and Arab or between Jew and Arab. Even today the seemingly pointless genocidal and suicidal battles rage in many places. Ceasefires are introduced and cancelled almost in the same moment; talks are organized on an international scale, but agreements are never reached. Civilians are blown to bits; hostages are taken; arms are bought and sold; and the whole ghastly drama lurches from act to act with no finale as yet even written. There is no peace, nor any prospect of any peace. But as Canon Ateek told me, this hasn't always been the case.

'Jews and Christian and Muslim Arabs have lived side by side as friendly communities for many centuries in past history. We have had very good periods of living as good neighbours; we shared life, land, and made friendships. A good part of our history has been shared by all of us where we shared things between ourselves on an equal basis. Now, when people come to me and say: What does God say about the position in which we find ourselves? I have to say to them that God is against oppression and injustice, and he does not approve of such a life for anyone. And those who try to use the Bible to justify such actions are misinterpreting Scripture, and understand neither the message of Scripture nor the message of the Bible. This is a very important aspect which I try to impress upon those who come to speak to me about the situation we have here in Palestine. I also say that we should never despair; that we should always trust in God, have faith in him and continue not only to pray but to work non-violently for a better future. As a Christian I cannot condone any violence, because there is so much we can do without violence against occupation. We can speak against it, we can proceed with certain peaceful protests to resist the occupation and try to bring the Israelis to their senses.'

Naim Ateek's latest book is called *Justice, and only Justice: a*

*Palestinian theology of liberation* (Orbis, 1989). I have always associated liberation theology, where the poor apply the gospel to their situation, with the countries of Latin America. Back in the early 1960s this new theology began to take root within newly created base communities in such countries as Brazil, Chile, Nicaragua and El Salvador.

'This book is an attempt to put that same theology into our context. We begin with our own situation and what is happening here. What are our people feeling? What are their sufferings? What is God saying to them and how can God help them today? Through the book I'm trying to throw a Christian perspective on our present-day situation, beginning where the people are. This is a theology very much biblically based because the Bible has been so much abused in the conflict; and it is an attempt also to really answer some of the difficulties, the problems and agonies of the Palestinian people. It's ironic that Christ came here, to this land, as the Prince of Peace, and yet there is so much conflict. Jesus Christ sacrificed so much for us through his death and resurrection in order to bring us peace, and to bring us closer to God and to each other: and yet here we are driven apart, away from each other, because of the conflict. So we hope that what Christ wanted to accomplish here will one day be accomplished in our land.'

Canon Ateek spoke very much from the heart, as did other Palestinians I met. They act and speak as an oppressed people who dearly wish for a peaceful settlement in a land they feel has been taken from under them, and they are helpless to bring about its restoration. To end our conversation in the English garden in the middle of Jerusalem, Canon Ateek quoted for me a prayer attributed to St Francis of Assisi which he'd recently used in one of his sermons. He felt this fairly summed up what he felt was the way forward for him and for all Palestinians:

> *Lord, make me an instrument of your peace:*
> *where there is hatred let me sow love;*
> *where there is injury, pardon;*

*where there is doubt, faith;*
*where there is despair, hope;*
*where there is darkness, light;*
*where there is sadness, joy.*
*O Divine Master, grant that I may not seek to be consoled, as to console;*
*to be understood as to understand;*
*to be loved as to love.*
*For it is in giving that we receive;*
*it is in pardoning that we are pardoned;*
*it is in dying that we are born to eternal life.*

On the way back to the Old City from St George's, I passed the famous Garden Tomb: a beautiful garden and, for many, a place more conducive to prayer and meditation than some of the more authentic holy places. I use the world 'authentic' because the Garden Tomb cannot be described as either historically or archaeologically correct. Its creation is recent, eccentric and very British.

It was first known after its founder, General Charles Gordon of Khartoum (1833–85), who became discontented with the church of the Holy Sepulchre and looked for an alternative. In 1883 he claimed he saw the shape of a skull in the caves near to the present-day Arab bus station. He honestly believed this to be the true Golgotha, the 'place of the skull' where Jesus was buried. In reality what he had found was a well-preserved first-century tomb. The small matter of its being so far from the city walls did not deter the general's enthusiasm. He wrote to Queen Victoria declaring he had found the authentic site of Calvary. Her Majesty replied and thanked the general for the information but stated she preferred to persevere in the tradition first established 'by our cousin Helena'! To be fair to Gordon, the gospels do mention the burial place of Jesus in a garden, and for many centuries the church of the Holy Sepulchre and its surroundings could in no way have represented anything remotely similar. Perhaps another reason for the Gordon tomb (later renamed the Garden Tomb) establishing itself as an alternative sepulchre was the Protestant desire to have a place of their own, separate from the overwhelming Orthodox and Catholic monopoly of most of the sites. Despite hard scientific evidence to the contrary, the Anglican Church in Jerusalem endorsed Gordon's findings and for a while supported the idea that this was the real burial place of Jesus. That support was eventually withdrawn, but still the garden remains a very popular place for many pilgrims who find the atmosphere more to their liking. Some described it as a quiet oasis in the midst of an exceedingly noisy city.

In the bright autumnal sunshine I walked down the Nablus Road and on towards the west side of the Old City. Before I left England I'd heard about the Anglican Christ Church, which has a rather unusual ministry. It's situated in the Armenian Quarter just inside the Jaffa Gate. Christ Church was built in 1849 by the London Jews Society, or the London Society for Promoting Christianity among the Jews. Today it's called the Christian Ministry among the Jews (CMJ). After the French Revolution, there was in England a strong millennialist feeling, and English Christians felt they were approaching the Last Days which would result in the return of Jesus. (Evidence for this belief, which goes back to mediaeval times, is based on the book of Revelation, chapter 20.) Before that second coming of Jesus, however, it was understood that certain conditions had to be met: the gospel had to be taken to all nations, and (more specifically) the gospel had to be taken back to the Jewish people, since they were the first to hear it. Add to that general belief the conviction of certain English Evangelical Christians that the Jewish people should have their land physically restored to them, again in the context of the Last Days. These firm beliefs led to the establishment of the London Society in 1809, and by 1820 the society had established a missionary station here in Jerusalem by the Jaffa Gate. Surprisingly enough, in those days there were only about 3,000 Jews in Jerusalem—mainly poor and very pious. Not the most promising scenario to begin such a revolutionary new idea in evangelism. But the English missionaries came and began their work of bringing Jesus to the Jews. In 1835 the society raised money to build Christ Church, a Reformed church where Protestant Christians would feel they had a place in Jerusalem. At that time the vast majority of Churches in the Holy City were either Roman Catholic or Orthodox. (Incredible as it may sound, it was forbidden for a Jew to go into the church of the Holy Sepulchre at that time.)

Thus Christ Church was built both to accommodate Protestants in Jerusalem, and also to serve as a place where those Jews who converted to Christianity could also come and worship. The Evangelicals were sensitive enough to fashion Christ Church in such a way as to make it amenable to Jewish worshippers as well as to themselves. It became known as the Jewish or Hebrew church as well as Christ Church. As you come into the church, it resembles a synagogue more than a church. On the back window is the legend, in Hebrew, 'God with us, the Spirit of God' accompanied by the star of David. It's an original window pock-marked now by shrapnel of the 1948 and 1967 wars. The same words, again in Hebrew, are repeated on the front window. The wooden area at the front of the church resembles the holy cupboard you'd find in any synagogue, where the Torah (the holy scrolls) are kept. On this cupboard are written the Apostles' Creed, the Lord's Prayer and the Ten Commandments. The altar, or table, at the front was made by Messianic Jews (the name describing those who have accepted Jesus into their lives) from the House of Industry.

Those Jews who lived in Jerusalem in the last century occupied their time mainly with studying the scriptures and were supported by Jewish colleagues overseas through a system of distribution. All monies were given out by the rabbis according to need. Those who became Messianic disqualified themselves from this assistance, and so the Christians organized alternative ways of supporting them. The House of Industry was one system where various trades were taught, and this altar, made of olive wood, was one of its products. Emblazoned on the front of the altar piece is the Hebrew word

*Emmanuel* (God with us). The point about Christ Church, and all it stands for, is that those Jews who wished—and still wish—to become Messianic, are able to do so without losing their Jewish cultural identity. Even though the church is built to accommodate Jewish believers, not many attend. I was told that those who do believe prefer to worship in private with one or two others, in a less public way. I understood that better when later I contacted some Messianic Jews who declined my invitation to be interviewed, explaining that they wished to maintain a low profile. I also spoke to a couple who had recently returned from East Africa under the Law of Return, a law by which all Jews are permitted to immigrate to Israel. Because this couple were Messianic—something they had decided upon whilst still in East Africa—they were denied full Israeli citizenship. The Israeli authorities informed them they were no longer considered to be Jewish.

Those who run the Christ Church mission explained to me that the church building is a symbol of the continuity between the Jewish faith and the Christian faith; one stems from the other and this place is a meeting point of Judaeo-Christianity. In the garden behind Christ Church I met Michael Bullman, Field Director of the Israel Trust of the Anglican Church. I was interested to know how the mission went about converting Jews to Christianity.

'I wouldn't put it that way', he replied. 'The way we see it is that a Jewish person should not be denied the knowledge of Jesus, who we believe is the Jewish Messiah. And if they do come to believe in someone who is, after all, a Jewish Messiah, that doesn't stop them being Jewish. We believe we are seeing a restoration of the early Church, in the time of Jesus, when the problem was not so much how can a Jew believe in Jesus, as how can a Gentile believe in him? If you read the Acts of the Apostles, this was the big problem at the council of Jerusalem: how could a Gentile believe in Jesus without being Jewish? They said you don't have to be Jewish to believe; and we're saying just the reverse—you don't have to forsake your Jewishness to believe.'

What difference does it make to the lives of those who become Messianic?

'It makes a great difference; and as a Christian myself I see that as a very great plus factor. Obviously it does create great problems in the Jewish community and in the families, we do realize that.'

I had to press the point that in the past missionaries in many countries have approached non-Christian cultures, converted some members, and totally alienated and isolated them from their own community. Many say this is an old-fashioned approach, and the way now is to bring about social reform where necessary; to demonstrate how Christianity can bring freedom from oppression and superstition; to show Christian examples; and let God do the rest. Head-counting is now not the way.

'Well, to that I would simply say that at the 1989 Lambeth Conference of Anglican Communion some of the African bishops, many from animist and Muslim environments, were very evangelistic and very keen to promote direct conversion to Christianity. Here at the mission we wouldn't countenance anything deceitful or underhand, but the plain truth is that we do believe in sharing openly the good news of Jesus in a sensitive and straightforward manner.'

Even though you know that you will cause social ostracization and family alienation for those Jews who do become believers?

'Yes. And we recognize this. We help people through those times. After all, Christianity is a costly business because the very centre of it is the death of Jesus on the cross. It's a hard thing; and again, one only has to look at the Acts of the Apostles to see how very often the arrival of the good news of Jesus, as well as bringing salvation, brought a lot of disturbance along with it. We don't wish for this, but we know that it very often comes as a by-product of spreading the Christian message. As to numbers: it isn't a vast amount of Jews who have accepted Jesus, but the number is increasing, both here and in other parts of the world. I should say there would be some 2,000–3,000 Messianic Jews in Israel at the moment.'

Perhaps one of the more contentious issues surrounding CMJ belief is the Jewish occupation of Israel as a fulfilment of biblical prophecy. Michael Bullman did emphasize that this should in no way deny Arab rights, or any other people's rights who live in Israel. Later I was to speak to a Palestinian Roman Catholic priest who wholeheartedly disagreed not only with CMJ's mission *per se*, but with its support of the Jewish occupation of Palestine and other territories.

I decided to cut through the Old City on my way back to Notre Dame. I more or less traced the route of the old Roman-Byzantine Cardo Maximus for a while, then turned north-west and left the Old City by the New Gate, opposite Notre Dame. As I approached the Centre up the rather steep incline to the entrance, I met a woman who told me she had lived in Jerusalem for sixteen years as a member of the Pontifical Mission for Palestine (1966–82). It was hot and she was rather breathless from the heat and the short climb, so we didn't chat for long. But what she did say to me has stayed with me: 'Pilgrims should not come to Jerusalem looking for consolation. It's the city of the cross, and not for the fainthearted. We are a suffering people on pilgrimage and here we have no abiding city, so be prepared for a difficult time.'

After dinner that evening, I'd arranged to see Fr Peter Madros, a Palestinian Roman Catholic who was parish priest at Beit Sahour (the Shepherds' Fields) out near Bethlehem. He was also lecturing at the diocesan seminary. The first thing which struck me about Fr Madros was his astonishing multilingual ability. I waited for him in the Centre's coffee shop, and since there were not many people around at nine in the evening (all exhausted pilgrims had long since retired), I recognized him as he stood at the reception desk. He is a slightly built man, with dark hair, sallow skin and he was wearing a dog-collar. He passed the time of evening in Arabic with the desk clerk; moved towards me and spoke to some people he knew in French; stopped at another table and addressed a party in Hebrew; then chatted to someone else in

Spanish. Minutes later when we introduced ourselves to each other, he spoke to me in perfect English with only the faintest trace of an accent. Later when I pursued his polyglot gift it transpired he was master in no less than sixteen languages, including Arabic, Hebrew, French, Spanish, English, Dutch, Italian (he trained in Rome) and Greek. When I pressed him on details he admitted to be more proficient in four other languages before his English, which was superb.

Fr Madros began by telling me about the blockade of his village of Beit Sahour for several weeks by the Israeli authorities. They refused to pay taxes to the military occupation forces, who they claimed had no right to receive them.

'The authorities tried diplomatically to persuade the people to pay the taxes. But there was no response. The issue escalated when the Israeli authorities began to take harsh measures against the population; they took away the tools of some people's trades, and even began confiscating domestic items from people's houses—like televisions, videos and fridges. These things were then auctioned off to raise the taxes. Those who head the national resistance in the occupied territories, since the *intifada*, always recommended that people did not pay their taxes. The people of Beit Sahour were carrying out this recommendation. On the other hand, other places were much more reluctant to obey this directive, because of the risks involved.'

As parish priest of the Roman Catholic community in Beit Sahour, did you encourage people to withhold payment of taxes?

'Well, thank God, I had no decision to make because the people had already decided on this course of action two years before I came to Beit Sahour, and people do not expect us to interfere in political affairs. However, I have condemned the taking away of people's tools by which they earn a living. This is taking food from people's mouths, and that is immoral. And I'm not the only one to speak out against this practice. Several members of the Israeli parliament said it was illegal, according to Israeli law, to deprive people of their livelihood in this way.

The Church has officially protested and it has made clear its solidarity with these people who justifiably defy the authorities. The problem, you see, is that our voice is never heard. We rely on outside help for support. Even political protestations by major powers around the world have not helped or improved the situation.'

When I asked Fr Madros for a comment on the general situation in Palestine at the moment, he was eager to talk of his 'Muslim brothers', notwithstanding the religious divide.

'We cannot disassociate ourselves from our brothers in the nation, who are Palestinian Muslims. Unfortunately we are not brothers according to our religions, although religions should tie people together through God. We Christians, however, are brothers in every respect except we do not share the same Creed, the same faith—although we all believe in one God. But we all share the same attitude with regard to Palestine. We are all hopeful that within our lifetime there will be a solution to the present difficulties.'

How did Fr Madros feel about the Holy Land seeming always to be in a state of conflict?

'If you read the history of "this blessed Holy Land"', he smiled, 'there's always been trouble here. But what I would say is that the sensitivity of Christians to the Holy Land has undergone a marked decrease over recent times. Whereas the Muslims and the Jews are very enthusiastic about the Holy Land. I believe that from the Western world Christians have been spoiled by a prosperous civilization, imagining that somehow God has no place in our lives. It seems to me that so many Christians know nothing of the Holy Land, and those who do know it, know nothing of the local Christians who live here. Pope Paul VI called them the 'living stones' [1 Peter 2:4], without whom we would have no more witnesses to be a continuation and a link with the time of the apostles. And without that Christian, local, Palestinian presence, those shrines, the holy places, would become museums.

'We Palestinians appreciate the fact that when we see pilgrims coming here, it does mean that they are interested in this Holy Land. But we need to see a lot more Christian pilgrims coming here, because we have the most holy places which are significant to us in their direct connection with Jesus' life and the early days of Christianity. The Jews and the Muslims support their holy places much more vigorously than we do, even though there can be no more holy places than *here* for Christians—the place where Jesus was actually born—in Bethlehem a mere fifteen-minute drive away. It's not normal therefore, that we have only 9,000 Christians in Jerusalem; and only a little over two per cent of the whole Palestinian population is Christian.'

So what do you want Christians to do?

'We want many more Christians to visit the Holy Land. Here are the fountains of belief; which means Jerusalem is the origin, the source, of their faith. And also Christians worldwide should be doing something to help Christians here in the Holy Land. We are dying out, emigrating, because of the difficult circumstances under which we live. I'm afraid to say that the ultimate and very sad conclusion to all this is that within twenty years there will be very few, or even no Christians left in Palestine. The holy places will be museums, and already the non-Christian guides are beginning to change the truth in order to spread their own political ideas.'

Fr Madros had kindly brought his latest book for me to read: *Faith and Scripture*, which is a treatment of how Catholic and Orthodox Christians can see how both Old and New Testaments can be used to support, verify and strengthen their faith on certain controversial issues. One chapter deals, for example, with the bodily resurrection of Jesus Christ; some believe that this was a symbolic resurrection and not to be understood in the literal sense. This book would help those with doubts to strengthen their faith in the actual bodily resurrection of Jesus with scriptural quotations and interpretations.

Since I was fresh from my visit to Christ Church, I asked Fr Madros for his opinion on the CMJ and Messianic Judaism.

'As a matter of principle, Jews should be the first to accept Christ because they have the complete Old Testament, especially the prophets who were the preparation for the coming of the Messiah. However, the historical factors like the hostility of Christians towards the Jews have not always fostered the opening of the eyes of the Jews. I say this of course in the light of my belief that Jesus of Nazareth is the Messiah. What we as Christians fear is that these Messianic Jews remain totally Jewish and take an entirely pro-Jewish approach to the scriptures. Although they say they believe in Jesus of Nazareth, they remain racist because they ignore the suffering of the Palestinians and voice unconditional support for the Jewish regime. They claim this is the Kingdom of God and the Jewish regime is part of God's chosen people. That to us is not in accord with the gospel. As Palestinians, therefore, we don't have too many contacts with Messianic Jews, unfortunately, because close association might be misconstrued as collaboration with Jewish authorities. It's very difficult for us to trust the new-found faith of the Messianics. We consider their belief to be incomplete because they don't accept Christ's divinity. They are not Judaeo-Christians.'

I felt that was a rather sad conclusion to our fascinating conversation. Mistrust seems to perpetuate itself in the land where I would have thought the opposite should be the case. It is to be hoped for the future that 'living stones' like Fr Peter Madros will, like the Church in Asia Minor when it too was suffering persecution, be built into a temple with Christ as 'a chosen precious cornerstone'.

I walked Fr Madros down to the car park in front of Notre Dame. We shook hands and he drove off towards his village of Beit Sahour. Fr Peter Madros has a big task before him.

## *Mr Husni Dhaher*

On the Friday I went to follow the stations of the cross with the Franciscan friars, which takes about an hour. I thought afterwards I'd wander through the narrow streets of the suq, the market place, which was closed in the afternoon at that time because of the *intifada*. The streets are not quite deserted: a few shops are open and there are always some people about. In a way it's as interesting when it's deserted as it is when it's teeming with people cluttering the walkways, buying and selling, shouting, eating and generally living the lives generations must have done for many thousands of years. Almost empty, it's a perfect way to absorb a little more of the Old City; and as I walked along I tried to imagine what it would have been like in the time of Jesus: Would the heat have been similar? Would the shadows have been the same? Perhaps he was hungry. Would he have bought a piece of fruit, or maybe had a drink from a water cart (hardly the Coca Cola it is today, but perhaps a particular fruit drink was popular in his time)?

What I hadn't taken into account was that every Friday Muslims pray at the mosque. The afternoon wore on and at about five I turned a corner and was confronted with a great moving mass of people completely filling the narrow passage way. They swept towards me in their thousands and it seemed useless to try to make progress against this human tide. I decided to take refuge in a doorway to observe them, and I was reminded of a crowd coming out of a football match. I then realized they had all been to pray at the Al Aqsa mosque. Muslims are devout people and take their religious faith seriously. In Israel today they number about 600,000, plus about 800,000 in the West Bank and the Gaza Strip, and the vast majority regularly attend the mosques.

By arrangement with the travel agent who was organizing our tour at the Jerusalem end, I managed to meet Husni Dhaher, a 52-year-old accountant and retired headmaster who's spent over 30 years in education. His village was Bethany, a place which figures greatly in the New Testament because of Jesus' friendship with Martha and Mary and Lazarus. Mr Dhaher knew the biblical story as well as I did and recounted it in some detail. As he spoke to me, I was impressed at the amount of Christian knowledge he had, and equally unimpressed at how little I knew about Islam. He described to me how Muslims honour all prophets, including Jesus, as well as Mary his mother. A Muslim should read all the holy books because though Muhammad was illiterate he encouraged people to read as much as they could. He spoke of how schools and universities had been closed down and how many parents sent their children to the United States and Europe for a decent education.

Like all religious Muslims, he prays five times a day, which reminded me how on more than one occasion our own bus driver thought nothing of getting out his prayer mat in a car park, turning to Mecca, and starting to pray. Husni Dhaher went on to relate how he believed in all the prophets, in angels, the day of judgement and every word written in the holy Quran. He thought Jerusalem one of the holiest places to Muslims everywhere because it is part of Islam.

'Once upon a time', he continued, 'Muslims used to pray facing Jerusalem and Al Aqsa mosque, and later it was changed to Mecca because God instructed Mohammad that this should be so. Jerusalem is part of our faith because the Prophet Muhammad went once to the Temple area and from there he ascended into heaven. He then returned to tell the people to pray five times a day to Almighty God. In those prayers we ask God to help us and we worship him. In the morning we have to pray before the sun breaks through; and then we pray in the middle of the day. The third occasion comes in the afternoon; then again in the evening at sunset; and finally we pray before going to bed. We worship only one God who created the universe and who controls our lives and our deaths. We don't drink alcohol, we don't eat pork, and we honour our parents. We don't believe in putting them in homes—we look after them ourselves, we feed them and smile at them to show them our respect.

'We have three important mosques which all Muslims must try to visit during their lifetime: the mosque at Mecca, the mosque at Medina where the prophet is buried, and Al Aqsa mosque here in Jerusalem. You see, Islam is based on the Five Pillars of Faith: the first is that there is no God other than

Allah, and Muhammad is his Prophet; secondly, to pray five times a day; thirdly, to give alms to poor people; number four, to fast during the month of Ramadan unless you are ill or travelling more than 81 kilometres; and finally the Haj: every Muslim must try to make a pilgrimage to Mecca at least once in his or her life and walk around the Kaaba, the great black stone.'

I wondered at this point if Mr Dhaher could have been one of the crowd I saw coming from the mosque the previous Friday?

'Yes certainly, I go every Friday and I pray because Friday is very important to us and we must not miss praying on this day more than three consecutive times without good reason. I feel very happy to go to pray. I listen to the imam who tells us that Muslims must be more united to save the holy places. We consider the Al Aqsa mosque is captured now and Muslims must set it free.'

But surely Muslim worshippers, like himself, were free to go to the mosque to pray whenever they chose?

'Not always. Sometimes we are interfered with and Israeli soldiers come inside with their arms and they fight with the people. The Israelis have captured it, even though it is part of our faith. And Muslims throughout the world should work towards the release of the mosque back to us, to whom it rightfully belongs. There is no doubt about it, we are a very depressed people because of the situation. Look at the West Bank. Once upon a time it was ruled by Arabs, and now it belongs to the Israelis; and now there is a dispute between us.'

But the Israelis claim that this land is their land, and they have right to it according to the Bible.

'Of course we do not accept this theory and this is precisely the dispute between the two parties, the Muslims and the Jews.'

What does the Quran tell you about being an oppressed people?

'Well first of all here we have to be patient. It's very important to Muslims because we believe that one day God will help us. We are waiting for this situation to end and we just have to wait. And when I go to pray at the mosque I pray that we may be set free; and I pray for prisoners who are not yet free. And of course I pray for members of my family. I ask for many good things for myself, my family and the whole of mankind.'

# DAY 5

## Emmaus, Caesarea and Galilee

For most Christians a pilgrimage to the Holy Land is a once in a lifetime experience. Money is saved for it, time is put aside for it, and—by the wise—a certain amount of study is done to prepare for it. Once there, the whole operation flashes before you in a kaleidoscopic blur of places, facts and figures, colours, noises and smells. There's so much to see and hear, and so little time to fit it all in. It's exhilarating, exciting, exhausting; but above all, it's memorable—perhaps one of the most memorable experiences you'll ever have. And strangely, it's an experience to be enjoyed and appreciated in retrospect, when the mind can take its time and recall the places and their atmosphere in more depth and detail, not unlike going through a set of photographs in the middle of a dreary winter after an enjoyable holiday in the sun. The Holy Land was certainly like all those things for me, prompted occasionally by a Bible reading during a church service; when a particular place is mentioned in the New Testament it really can come alive as the mind makes the connection between the reading and the actual place itself.

### Emmaus

This was the morning we set out for Emmaus at Abu Ghosh, complete with our luggage packed deep inside the belly of the bus. Our pilgrim journey was now taking us north, to the country where Jesus spent most of his life in seclusion at Nazareth before beginning his three-year ministry in Galilee. The most direct route would have been north through Nablus; but because of *intifada* trouble we had to take a different route—to the west almost as far as Tel Aviv, then north and parallel with the coast to Caesarea. This meant that Emmaus at Abu Ghosh was on our route out of Jerusalem. As with all visits on a pilgrimage such as this, our Abu Ghosh stop was brief, but somehow it made an impression on many of us, and we spoke about it for some days after. Certainly for me the vivid recollection of that church has remained in my mind, and will remain with me for a long time to come. We arrived after a drive of about eight miles due west on the main road to Tel Aviv. Again, as with so many places in the Holy Land, the authenticity of Abu Ghosh as the Emmaus mentioned in the New Testament can only be guessed at. The fact is that there are three sites from which to choose, all claiming to be Emmaus, the place where the risen Christ first showed himself to those who knew him.

Latrun, past Abu Ghosh and further along the road towards Tel Aviv, was popularly believed in Byzantine times to be the place the risen Christ was first seen. The book of Maccabees mentions it a couple of times as a strategically important site between Jerusalem and the coastal plain. In the seventh century a plague wiped the village out, but because of its strategic position the Crusaders revived its fortunes and built a fortress there. For centuries it was the Arab village of Imwas, also called Emmaus. In 1967 however, during the Six Day War, the villagers were moved out, their village destroyed and turned into what is today called Canada Park, a picnic area.

Qubeiba, about eight miles north-west of Jerusalem off the Ramallah road, is yet another possible site for Emmaus. This spot has been venerated by many as the true Emmaus since 1500, and every Easter Monday pilgrims come here to read the Emmaus story and witness the blessing of bread by the Custodian of the Holy Land. A main Roman road ran through Qubeiba alongside which Arabs built their houses. Later, in the twelfth century, the Canons of the Holy Sepulchre established a village here and probably a resting place for pilgrims on their way to Jerusalem from the coast. At a little over eight miles, Qubeiba is the nearest site to Jerusalem and comes close to Luke's estimated 60 stadia (seven miles; 24:13). Abu Ghosh and Latrun are a little further away from Jerusalem, more to the south, but all are within a day's walking distance of the holy city. So in a way, all these sites are possibles, and the one we happened upon was Abu Ghosh.

This was the site first favoured by the Crusaders and its name is taken from a local Arab sheik, a ne'er-do-well who stopped all the caravans and exacted huge tolls from them before allowing them to proceed either to or from Jerusalem. Going into the church grounds was like entering a 'secret garden'. We passed from a noisy, busy street into the peace and calm of a quite lovely, serene and colourful garden. High up on the hill, backing the complex, is a gigantic statue of the Virgin and Child (about 50 feet high), sometimes referred to as Our Lady of the Covenant. It's the site of the Old Testament village of Qiryat Yearim, the last resting place of the Ark of the Covenant before King David decided it was more appropriate to transport it to Jerusalem (2 Samuel 6:3–5). 'They transported the ark of God on a new cart and brought it out of Abinadab's house which is on the hill. Uzzah and Ahio, the sons of Abinadab, drove the cart, Uzzah walked alongside the ark of God and Ahio went in front. David and the whole House of Israel danced before Yahweh with all their might, singing to the accompaniment of harps, lyres, tambourines, sistrums and cymbals.'

The church at Abu Ghosh is Crusader built, and incorporates a stone marking a camp of the Roman Tenth Legion. The soaring, vaulted Crusader arches lend themselves to perfect acoustics, and before we put them to the test, Andrew read the story of Emmaus.

LUKE 24:13–35

Now that very same day, two of them were on their way to a village called Emmaus, seven miles from Jerusalem, and they were talking together about all that had happened. And it happened that as they were talking together and discussing it, Jesus himself came up and walked by their side; but their eyes were prevented from recognizing him. He said to them, 'What are all these things that you are discussing as you walk along?' They stopped, their faces downcast.

Then one of them, called Cleopas, answered him, 'You must be the only person in Jerusalem who does not know the things that have been happening there these last few days.' He asked, 'What things?' They answered, 'All about Jesus of Nazareth, who showed himself a prophet powerful in action and speech before God and the whole people; and how our chief priests and our leaders handed him over to be sentenced to death, and had him crucified. Our own hope had been that he would be the one to set Israel free. And this is not all: two whole days have now gone by since it all happened; and some women from our group have astounded us: they went to the tomb in the early morning, and when they could not find the body, they came back to tell us they had seen a vision of angels who declared he was alive. Some of our friends went to the tomb and found everything exactly as the women had reported, but of him they saw nothing.'

Then he said to them, 'You foolish men! So slow to believe all that the prophets have said! Was it not necessary that the Christ should suffer before entering into his glory?' Then, starting with Moses and going through all the prophets, he explained to them the passages throughout the Scriptures that were about himself.

When they drew near to the village to which they were going, he made as if to go on; but they pressed him to stay with them saying, 'It is nearly evening and the day is almost over.' So he went in to stay with them. Now while he was with them at table, he took the bread and said the blessing; then he broke it and handed it to them. And their eyes were opened and they recognized him, but he had vanished from their sight. Then they said to each other, 'Did not our hearts burn within us as he talked to us on the road and explained the Scriptures to us?'

They set out that instant and returned to Jerusalem. There they found the Eleven assembled together with their companions, who said to them, 'The Lord has indeed risen and appeared to Simon.' Then they told their story of what had happened on the road and how they had recognized him at the breaking of bread.

It's a remarkable story when you think about it: Jesus had

been put to death in a most violent and horrible way, and his followers—including the apostles and the women—really didn't know what was going to happen next. They had some vague idea that he said he would 'rise from the dead', but exactly what that meant couldn't have been clear to them. On the morning after the Sabbath it had been discovered that the entrance to the tomb had been tampered with, and the grave was empty. More confusion still! And now, two reliable men who had been walking near to the village of Emmaus report this fantastic story that they have been with Jesus, the man they all had seen put to death and laid in his tomb. You can imagine the barrage of questions: What did he look like? What was he doing out at Emmaus? Why didn't you recognize him immediately? When you say vanished, what do you mean exactly? And so on. As we know, Jesus made himself known on several subsequent occasions, but I suppose it must have taken a while before even his apostles really began to understand and believe that he had risen again, as he said he would. After the New Testament story, Andrew read from his own book of readings.

Draw near to us, Lord,
here at Emmaus.
Here
and everywhere
make yourself known to us
in the breaking of bread.

Risen Lord, who on the first Easter day drew near to your two disciples on the Emmaus road, and at evening stayed with them in their village home: be our unseen companion along the daily journey of our life, and at the ending of the day come and abide with us in our dwellings; for your love's sake.
*Contemporary Parish Prayers*

After we attempted to take full advantage of the remarkable acoustics at Abu Ghosh church, we walked around the garden. French Benedictine monks and nuns care for the church, and we saw several of them working in the kitchen garden behind the more decorative area beside the church. At the end of one wall there's a water pitcher set on the corner; it's surrounded by purple bougainvillaea and other colourful flowers, all contriving to create an atmosphere of peace and tranquillity. And it works: once we'd got the Emmaus story firmly fixed in our minds the whole setting seemed to fit together. Someone bought an audio cassette of the monks and nuns singing Gregorian plainchant in the wonderful chapel. I also have a copy now and it's one of the best souvenirs I have of the Holy Land trip. When I listen to the singing, I'm taken back to that garden at Abu Ghosh and the Emmaus story comes alive. I'd like to return there one day.

We left Emmaus–Abu Ghosh in the late morning and headed for our northern destination of Caesarea via the outskirts of Tel Aviv. The journey was uneventful, hot and rather bumpy. (Try to sit towards the front of the coach/bus—bumps are absorbed better there!) The motorways we travelled along were adequate, and had certainly nothing like the volume of traffic which blights the British and Continental roadways. At one point a cry of astonishment went up and our attention was drawn to a full-blown cricket match on a green and grassy pitch just across the road! We sped on, even though watching a couple of overs seemed like a good idea at the time.

## Caesarea

By our route it took about two hours to get to the port of Caesarea, which lies just over 30 miles north of Tel Aviv and about 25 miles south of Haifa. (This is not Caesarea Philippi, which is much further north, inland: see Day Nine.) With just a short stretch of the imagination, it isn't difficult to see just what magnificent builders they were 2,000 years ago. The town was given by Augustus to Herod the Great in 30 BC. In those days Jaffa (Tel Aviv) had served as the main port, but Herod decided to make Caesarea (Caesar's Town) something really grand; he sank thousands of cubic metres of stone under the water to create a harbour, some 50 feet long, 9 feet high and 10 feet wide to a depth of 20 fathoms; he built a palace, an amphitheatre (still used today), and a magnificent temple dedicated to Augustus. When the Romans took over, they made Caesarea the capital city, which it remained for 600 years. St Paul makes mention of this place several times as he passed through on his missionary journeys. On his way to Rome to be tried, he was imprisoned here. The port decreased in importance and activity, and in 640 it fell to the Arabs. At the beginning of the twelfth century the Crusaders took Caesarea, where it's said the Holy Grail was discovered—the cup Jesus used at the Last Supper. Look out for the stone which bears the name of Pontius Pilate—his only mention in stone. Origen, one of the early Christian Fathers, was ordained here in the third century, and Eusebius the historian was bishop here in the following century.

A good third of the harbour is now under water and a lot of underwater archaeology is now in progress. The main excavations were done by Italians in the 1950s, and the site, as we saw it, was littered with masonry treasures exposed over recent years. They have uncovered massive pillars, slabs of stone and decorated pieces of masonry, and all of these so large you have to marvel at the way the engineering of the time was able to manage such huge projects without benefit of sophisticated hydraulics, electrical or steam power. Andrew waxed lyrical about the amphitheatre which he had attended for concerts: 'You're looking out to sea, and the sun sets over the Mediterranean at about seven in the evening, and that lovely red ball sinks towards the skyline as you take your seat for the concert.' There are even devilishly clever fish-ponds which were natural traps for the fish: once they swam in from the sea, they couldn't get out again. All people had to do was fry the fish which was there for the taking!

We then wandered round and saw some Crusader church

ruins; one entrance to the fortress is a particularly fine example of Crusader architecture, as are the remnants of the shops. We walked down whole and complete streets which were so solidly put together, they felt and looked new.

## Bet Shean

From Caesarea we drove inland a good distance to the town of Bet Shean, about 75 miles north of Jerusalem and 20 miles south of Nazareth. The land, close to the Jordan, is fertile around this area, which accounts for the fact that it has been continuously inhabited since the Stone Age over 5,000 years ago. The *tel*, or mound, is 80 metres high and contains the remains of eighteen cities, one built on top of the other as they were renewed. Because of excellent fortifications, it was able to resist becoming part of Israel in David's time, and only did so later under his son Solomon. Saul, the first king of Israel, was killed by the Philistines at the battle of Gilboa (1 Samuel 31), a few miles to the south-west of Bet Shean. His decapitated body was then brought here and displayed on the ramparts.

The main reason for visiting Bet Shean, however, is to see two remarkable things: the spectacular Roman theatre which is probably the best preserved in the country, and the synagogue floor mosaic at the Bet Alpha kibbutz just west of the town. The Roman basalt theatre, built around AD 200, is quite breathtaking; as you go in through any one of the many entrances behind the seating, it's just like going into a modern football stadium. The Latin name for these archways was *vomitoria*: that is, the quickest exit in case of necessity! Apparently some of the 'entertainment' down in the arena and on the stage was so grisly (fights to the death between people, animals, animals and people etc.) it was too much for some—particularly after a not unusual fifteen-course meal! The tiers look down onto a massive stage flanked by huge stone pillars across the back. The auditorium even had a sound-amplifying system of shell-shaped reflectors and tubes. Beyond the stage are excavations which have only been opened to the public for a short time and are well worth a quick visit. We strolled along wide pavements which were streets centuries ago, we saw storehouses, huge columns lying down like stranded whales, and some resurrected by excavators and restored to their original positions.

The synagogue at Bet Alfa kibbutz dates from the time of Justin I in the sixth century and was discovered in 1928 when land, now belonging to the kibbutz, was being irrigated. Experts were called in to excavate, and painstaking efforts revealed a most remarkable and intricate mosaic the size of a squash court. We filed along a raised balcony round the edges of the mosaic which we could see some feet below us. It's a wonderful and detailed piece of work and should not be missed. It's divided into three panels: the main feature of the bottom section shows Abraham sacrificing Isaac, and God's hand coming out of heaven with the Hebrew words 'hold thy hand'; alongside there's the ram in the thicket. The centre and largest panel is given over to the signs of the zodiac. Although these signs were, and still are, pagan symbols, the rabbis of the time were compelled to include them because their congregations, keen on fortune-telling, demanded it. The depiction of animals and humans, not in accord with Jewish religious practice, indicates the liberal attitude of these particular Jews in the sixth century. The upper panel depicts Jewish religious artefacts or symbols like the menorah, the Lion of Judah, and a space top left where the Ark would have stood. It's well lit and well presented, and certainly worth the slight detour from Bet Shean to see it.

## *Tiberias*

It had been a long day, and we'd travelled further than at any time since we'd arrived in the Holy Land. We'd seen a lot and by late afternoon we were glad to be at our hotel in Tiberias. And best of all we were on the shore of the sea of Galilee. Years before, when I visited Jerusalem, I'd been very keen to get up here but it wasn't to be. Now there I was, on the north shore of the sea. How familiar that word Galilee was to me and the rest of the group; how many times had we heard it in the gospel. Now we were going to see it, to be at those places Jesus knew well when he was growing up with Joseph and Mary at Nazareth, just 12 miles south-west of Tiberias.

We settled into our rooms, met for dinner and discussed the day's events. From the balcony of my room I could see the smooth surface of the sea of Galilee which I found very exciting. I could see car lights moving on the road running around the edge, and the odd boat light winking far out in the water. It's called a 'sea' but actually it's a big lake: 15 miles long and about 8 miles wide. On one or two subsequent evenings, the moon would cast its pale light across the still water as a cool breeze wafted into the open window and gently filled the curtains. Those of us who felt inclined walked down a steep hill to Tiberias town and the harbour. It's a popular seaside resort, complete with a spa, lots of restaurants and ice-cream parlours. I found it loud, brash and a bit of fun. Café touts would energetically try to lure us into eating at their (rather expensive) establishments along the marina where many luxury pleasure craft were moored. It was a good walk and we needed it after so many hours in the coach.

Jesus would have known Tiberias as a 'new town' since it was built in his lifetime by Herod the Great's son Herod Antipas, in honour of the Emperor Tiberius. Since it was a wholly Roman settlement, Jesus probably hardly even went there. It's been famous down the ages for its fish. Eating the 'St Peter's fish' all visitors are encouraged to have at a seaside restaurant on the opposite side to Tiberias at En Gev is quite an occasion. You have to have a lot of patience, though, with a piece of very bony but quite tasty fish.

After the fall of Jerusalem in AD 70 many Jews made Tiberias their home and it became a centre of Jewish learning in the third century. It was here that the Talmud, the book of Jewish Law, was completed. Peter and Andrew would have known Tiberias well as local fishermen down from Capernaum, less than 10 miles further north along the coast. Obviously Jesus came to know Peter and Andrew, as well as James, John and Philip who came from Bethsaida (a town whose whereabouts is yet to be discovered). His whole Galilean ministry was focused around the sea and those who showed interest in what he was preaching were the fishermen, who witnessed three miracles all connected with the water by which they made their living: the great catch of fish when the nets almost broke (Luke 5), Jesus rebuking the wind and stilling the storm (Luke 7), and Jesus walking on the water (Matthew 14).

# DAY 6

## *Capernaum*

Capernaum was our first stop from Tiberias, just 12 miles to the north of the shore of the Galilean sea, near to where the river Jordan flows into it. In Jesus' time it served as a fish market for several fishing villages in the vicinity, and most likely other goods came here for sale and distribution. Canon Ron Brownrigg in his detailed guide to the Holy Land *Come, See the Place* (Hodder & Stoughton, 1988) paints a very lively and colourful picture of what life was like in the busy market-town-port of Capernaum during Jesus' time:

> Half a mile of lakeside ruins and a considerable depth of water witness to the harbour and warehouse installations of long ago. The town was in fact one vast seabound market place, a cosmopolis teeming with merchants from Phoenicia and Damascus, Greeks and Romans from the Ten Towns, and wholesale buyers from Jerusalem. Less conspicuous among the jostling crowds along the jetties were the stevedores and shipwrights and local fisher-folk—sorting fish, pickling, packing, mending nets, making sails, painting boats. Along the coastal way, which crossed into Herod Philip's territory at the fords of the Jordan less than a mile away, rolled the ox-carts heaped high with vegetables and fruit—to the sound of camel bells. Camel-trains roped nose to tail, plodded through the dust or stood bored yet patient under vast loads in the thick of the traffic jam. Ubiquitous donkeys and mules pushed through, like mopeds at traffic lights. Every now and then, amidst the crush, the plumed helmet of a legionary, the black gown of a rabbi, Pharisee or scribe; and the brass badge of the publican, each about his own particular business in the melée of men and animals.

Jesus made Capernaum, sometimes called 'his own city', the base for his Galilean ministry. It was a border town: the river

Jordan was the natural line between Galilee and the territory of Philip the Tetrarch. There was a customs post here, where Matthew (Levi) worked as a customs and excise official, collecting revenues before he decided to follow Jesus. According to his own account in his own gospel, Matthew's voluntary redundancy from the tax office was so sudden—one wonders how many passed through tax-free until a replacement was found!

MATTHEW 9:9

As Jesus was walking from there [having cured the paralytic] he saw a man named Matthew sitting at the tax office, and he said to him, 'Follow me'. And he got up and followed him.

The place of most interest to pilgrim visitors is the house of Peter and the synagogue area. A large part of the complex is now owned and administered by the Franciscan friars, who took charge at the beginning of this century as official custodians of the holy places. Part of the site is owned by the Orthodox. Many revered spots in the Holy Land have been built over with churches and basilicas and other monuments which tend to obscure, and sometimes destroy, what was there in the first instance. And so it is with the house of Peter. The Franciscans have built a huge church above the site, reliably thought to be the place where St Peter, the fisherman, lived and plied his trade on the sea of Galilee. The Franciscan excavators found crosses inscribed on the walls, fish hooks embedded in the floor, pilgrim inscriptions (dating from various periods) of those who had visited and venerated the house as that belonging to St Peter. Unfortunately the general public is not admitted into the house, something I greatly regretted.

There's early evidence that this was used as a house-church in the second and third centuries, after which it was turned into a basilica. Finally, by the fifth century it was a large octagonal basilica, used as a church. So if you ask yourself the question: Why should one of these comparatively insignificant council houses in Capernaum have been designated for special treatment, and evolved from a house-church, via a square basilica to a rather grand octagonal basilica by the fifth century? The answer is that this was always believed to have been the house of St Peter, the chief apostle. Jesus would have slept here many times.

I found it fascinating to stand looking out to the sea, with the synagogue behind me, and the remains of the sort of house Jesus stayed in while up at Capernaum from Nazareth. I was astounded to see they were nothing more than humble, dry-stone-walled shacks, connected to each other by tiny open spaces or courtyards. They were so tiny and so ordinary; yet this is where Jesus stayed, and he doubtless came from a similar home in Nazareth! Naturally they were roofless now, and in those early days they would have had light roofing on them of woven palms, sufficient for the clement weather in the region. The easily removable roof immediately reminded me of the paralytic in Mark's gospel (2:1–12).

When he returned to Capernaum, some time later word went round that he was in the house; and so many people collected that there was no room left, even in the front of the door. He was preaching the word to them when some people came bringing him a paralytic carried by four men, but as they could not get the man to him through the crowd, they stripped the roof over the place where Jesus was; and when they had made an opening, they lowered the stretcher on which the paralytic lay.

And as we know, Jesus cured the man—having first offered to forgive him his sins. That gospel story shows how these houses, really little more than crude huts made of black basalt stone, were constructed. It also got me thinking about the ordinariness of Jesus, his way of life and that of those around him. Somehow between them, from an unknown corner of the great Roman empire, they managed to launch Christianity, to spread all over the world. It may have been a little naive to imagine that Jesus lived somewhere grand, but I was hardly prepared for this. Judging from the size of those huts there was barely room for a man to lie down, much less for a whole family to sleep. And where did they cook, take recreation, have conversation etc.? Of course, the weather is such that most activities took place out of doors, and being inside was much less important than for those who lived in colder, less easy climates. Populations were tiny in those days compared with now, and the handful of people who lived at Capernaum probably knew Jesus well and on a very personal basis.

The synagogue gave me a great thrill. It's a very well-restored building and dates back to the early centuries. The substantial remains, in their bright, white limestone, indicate just what a magnificent building it must have been: in a totally different and far superior league from the black basalt surrounding dwellings. Much of the carved masonry scattered at the front of the building is the remains from the main façade. When the Franciscans first discovered this synagogue, there was great excitement because some thought this could be the place where Jesus himself worshipped. However, it later became clear that though this was on the same *site* as the synagogue in Jesus' time, it was built later—probably around 350. Some of the detail on the decoration reveals bunches of grapes, pomegranates, the star of David, and a depiction of the Ark of the Covenant on its wheels as it was carried around by the Israelites in their desert wanderings before it was eventually taken in triumph to Jerusalem. There's also a Roman milestone indicating the Via Maris (the Way of the Sea), on the road to the south towards Jerusalem. You'll see a mosaic of a fishing boat, the shape of which ties in nicely with a first-century fishing smack discovered in 1986 nearby at Kibbutz Nof Ginnosar, south of Capernaum on the coast road. The way the boat was constructed, plus the cooking pot and the oil-lamp found inside it, makes its first-century date indisputable. The boat, 7 feet wide and 27 feet long, is still in the kibbutz, immersed in a special solution to prevent it from disintegrating. For religious reasons, synagogues were always built higher than surrounding buildings, and if you look closely at the base of it, there's a darker foundation ridge running along the nearside. This foundation is said to be part of the synagogue Jesus would have known and worshipped in when he was visiting Peter and the others.

Once the party ahead of us left the synagogue, we then moved in, sat down on the same stone benches as thousands had done before us, and Andrew read two short passages from the New Testament:

MARK 1:21–28

They went as far as Capernaum, and at once on the Sabbath Jesus entered the synagogue and began to teach. And his teaching made a deep impression on them because, unlike the scribes, he taught them with authority.

And at once in the synagogue there was a man with an unclean spirit, and he shouted, 'What do you want with us, Jesus of Nazareth? Have you come to destroy us? I know who you are: the Holy One of God.' But Jesus rebuked it saying, 'Be quiet! come out of him!' And the unclean spirit threw the man into convulsions and with a loud cry went out of him. The people were so astonished that they started asking one another what it all meant, saying, 'Here is a teaching that is new, and with authority behind it: he gives orders even to unclean spirits and they obey him.' And his reputation at once spread everywhere, through all the surrounding Galilean countryside.

And at once on leaving the synagogue, he went with James and John straight to the house of Simon and Andrew. Now Simon's mother-in-law was in bed and feverish, and at once they told him about her. He went in to her, took her by the hand and helped her up. And the fever left her and she began to serve them.

MATTHEW 4:12–17

Hearing that John had been arrested he withdrew to Galilee, and leaving Nazara he went and settled in Capernaum, beside the lake, on the borders of Zebulun and Naphtali. This was to fulfil what was spoken by the prophet Isaiah:

'Land of Zebulun! Land of Naphtali!
Way of the sea beyond Jordan.
Galilee of the nations!
The people that lived in darkness
have seen a great light;
on those who lived in a country of shadow dark as death
a light has dawned.'

From then onwards Jesus began his proclamation with the message, 'Repent, for the king of Heaven is close at hand.'

What stunning texts, especially read and heard in the very place where many of these events actually took place. That's the privilege of going to the Holy Land. Andrew then read from his own text.

*'Let's go home.'*
*I wonder how many times you said that, Lord,*
*when you came back to Capernaum with your disciples?*

*And yet it wasn't your home.*
*The nearest to home for you was Nazareth,*
*but even that wasn't home;*
*for you had no home,*
*nowhere to lay your head*
*except the wild places of Galilee*
*and the homes of your friends.*

*No, Lord, this was the home of Peter.*
*He shared it with you*
*and it became your home—for the moment.*
*This was your home-base in Galilee.*
*Here at Capernaum*
*you taught in the synagogue*
*and healed the people.*

*Lord, I want my home to be like this
simple home of Peter.
A base, a centre of love,
of teaching and healing.*


*Visit, we beseech thee, O Lord, our homes, and drive far from them all the snares of the enemy; let the holy angels dwell to preserve us in peace; and may thy blessing be upon us evermore; through Jesus Christ our Lord.*

From the Order of Compline


That experience, and seeing the humble houses there near the lakeside, made the whole of the pilgrimage worth while. Take a look at the skyline with its mountains and valleys; it's exactly the same now as Jesus would have seen it 2,000 years ago.

## Church of Peter's Primacy

A ten-minute drive south of Capernaum, still on the edge of the sea, is Tabgha, and adjoining that the church of St Peter's Primacy. The church, or chapel really, is very modern and rather stylish. It was built by the Franciscans in 1933, but pilgrims have been coming here for many centuries, from the time when the Christian pilgrim Egeria, a nun, visited in the fourth century and recorded something of what she saw. It's a natural fishing harbour, and if you look at the rock on which the church rests, you'll see stone steps leading down from it into the lake. In New Testament times the water would have been higher than it is now, and even within the last ten years a difference has been noticed. This was the place often referred to by early Christians as the 'place of the coals', where the risen Jesus had prepared grilled fish for his disciples' breakfast as they came ashore.

## JOHN 21:9–14

As soon as they came ashore they saw that there was some bread there and a charcoal fire with fish cooking on it. Jesus said, 'bring some of the fish you have just caught.' Simon Peter went aboard and dragged the net ashore, full of big fish, one hundred and fifty-three of them; and in spite of there being so many the net was not broken. Jesus said to them, 'Come and have breakfast.' None of the disciples was bold enough to ask, 'Who are you?' They knew quite well it was the Lord. Jesus then stepped forward, took the bread and gave it to them, and the same with the fish. This was the third time that Jesus revealed himself to the disciples after rising from the dead.

Originally there was a small Byzantine church on this site which was destroyed by the Persians. The Crusaders then rebuilt it in much the same proportions as it has today. Later the Franciscans erected this beautiful chapel, with its startling stained glass. Note the rather dramatic altar, which is part of the rock which projects through the back of the chapel. Silence is strictly preferred inside. Outside, to the side of the chapel, is an altar with ample seating, where I watched a large group from Brazil singing hymns and hearing Mass.

This is the natural harbour where Jesus would have pulled out from the shore in a boat to speak to the crowds who flocked to hear him as his fame began to spread on the shores of Galilee. Pope Paul VI made a visit here in 1964, the place where Peter, the first Pope, was forgiven after three times denying Jesus. Presumably, when they had eaten breakfast, Jesus thought it time to clear up one or two problems concerning Peter and some of his fundamental beliefs.

## JOHN 21:15–19

When they had eaten, Jesus said to Simon Peter, 'Simon son of John, do you love me more than the others do? He answered, 'Yes, Lord, you know I love you.' Jesus said to him, 'Feed my lambs.' A second time he said to him, 'Simon son of John, do you love me?' He replied, 'Yes, Lord, you know I love you.' Jesus said to him, 'Look after my sheep.' Then he said to him a third time, 'Simon son of John, do you love me?' Peter was hurt when he asked him a third time, 'Do you love me?' and said, 'Lord, you know everything; you know I love you.' Jesus said to him 'Feed my sheep.' ... And after this he said to him 'Follow me.'

### *Tabgha* (or *Heptapegon: Seven Springs*)

This is next door to the church of Peter's Primacy; until around 350 the early Judaeo-Christians of Capernaum venerated this spot (then a large rock) as the place where Jesus fed the five thousand with the loaves and the fishes. The rock was used as the altar of the church, believed to have been the table Jesus used to distribute the food. Later, in the fifth century, a larger Byzantine church was built, again incorporating the same rock as an altar. Underneath was a mosaic of loaves and fishes, covering much of the floor of the church, including the flora and fauna of Galilee of the time. Thanks to the Benedictine monks who came here in the 1930s, this spectacular mosaic is preserved for pilgrims to see. The Benedictines covered the area with a small wooden church, complete with a corrugated iron roof, until 1980. The mosaic was then removed piece by piece (and when you see it you'll realize what a tremendous task that must have been), and the present church was built as an exact replica of the original Byzantine church. The mosaic was carefully and accurately replaced, and now we have the wonderful privilege of seeing this reconstructed marvel just as pilgrims many centuries ago would have seen: the loaves and fishes mosaic in the sanctuary (see the mullet or St Peter's fish); and the local wildlife: flamingos, peacocks, snakes, doves, ducks in a lotus flower, geese, and lots more. In John's gospel we hear how Jesus, who had gathered the inevitable crowd around him because he was curing the sick, wondered how all these people were going to be fed (and 5,000 was a vast number in those days) as many had come long distances to see and hear him.

JOHN 6:5–13

Looking up, Jesus saw the crowds approaching and said to Philip, 'Where can we buy some bread for these people to eat?' He said this only to put Philip to the test; he himself knew exactly what he was going to do. Philip answered, 'Two hundred denarii would not buy enough to give them a little piece each.' One of his disciples, Andrew, Simon Peter's brother, said, 'Here is a small boy with five barley loaves and two fish; but what is that among so many?' Jesus said to them, 'Make the people sit down.' There was plenty of grass there, and as many as five thousand men sat down. Then Jesus took the loaves, gave thanks, and distributed them to those who were sitting there; he then did the same with the fish, distributing as much as they wanted. When they had eaten enough, he said to the disciples, 'Pick up the pieces left over, so that nothing is wasted.' So they picked them up and filled twelve large baskets with scraps left over from the meal of five barley loaves.


Because of its splendour, the church is very busy; so you have to keep moving—and as silently as possible.

# DAY 7

## *Nazareth and Mount Tabor*

Less than 20 miles south-west of Tiberias is Nazareth, the town where Jesus is said to have spent 30 years of his life before commencing his public ministry. The name Nazareth is only mentioned in the New Testament: by Matthew, Luke, John and in Acts. But it seems they don't all agree as to where Mary and Joseph lived before the birth of Jesus. Matthew (2:1) indicates it was Bethlehem: 'After Jesus had been born in Bethlehem during the reign of King Herod ...'. Whereas Luke (2:4–5) says it definitely was Nazareth: 'So Joseph set out from the town of Nazareth in Galilee for Judaea, to David's town called Bethlehem, since he was of David's house and line ...'. According to Fr Jerome Murphy-O'Connor in his book *The Holy Land*, it is more likely that Matthew is correct; Joseph was Judaean (Bethlehem), not a Galilean (Nazareth). When both Joseph and Mary were threatened by Herod, who wanted the baby king slaughtered, it would have been more natural for the Holy Family to return to Nazareth, from Bethlehem where Jesus was born, if that had been their home. As we know, they fled instead to Egypt for refuge—a country Judaeans of the time knew to be a safe place. In Luke's gospel (1:39–40) we read how Mary went to visit her cousin Elizabeth, Zachary's wife: 'Mary set out at that time and went quickly as she could into the hill country to a town in Judah ...'. That Mary went to a town 'in Judah' meant it couldn't have been far from Bethlehem. Had Mary lived up in Nazareth, it's hardly likely she would have made such a long journey, about three days walking—and certainly not alone. It's possible Joseph moved north to Nazareth, after the birth of Jesus, to get work. He was an artisan—a carpenter or a builder—and at the time Herod Antipas was starting to construct his capital city Sepphoris and needed to employ skilled men. Jesus was probably so young at the time of his parents' move that Nazareth became his home town.

It's curious that little is heard of about Nazareth after its initial mention in the New Testament; the whole focus of attention comes to rest on Jerusalem and the Galilee area where certainly more dramatic events took place during Jesus' three-year public ministry. Various writers down the centuries mention Nazareth in passing, but not to any great extent. For the modern pilgrim, it's a rather disappointing place; nothing of the small and sleepy village where you might expect Jesus to have been raised. It's a large town now, noisy and dusty, with lots of traffic and an air of dilapidation and shabbiness. There's a population of some 35,000, mostly Arab Christians.

We started at the basilica of the Annunciation, an enormous church built to commemorate the moment when Mary was told by the Angel Gabriel that she was to become the mother of God.

LUKE 1:31–35

'You are to conceive in your womb and bear a son, and you must name him Jesus. He will be great and he will be called the Son of the Most High. The Lord God will give him the throne of his ancestor David; he will rule over the House of Jacob for ever and his reign will have no end.' Mary said to the angel, 'But how can this come about, since I have no knowledge of man?' The angel answered, 'The Holy Spirit will come upon you, and the power of the Most High will cover you with its shadow. And so the child will be holy and will be called the Son of God.' ... Mary said, 'You see before you the Lord's servant, let it happen to me as you have said.' And the angel left her.

The site of the basilica was venerated by Judaeo-Christians from the first two centuries, and covered the cave where Mary was said to have been visited by the Angel Gabriel. It's some 300 years later that we hear anything more about Nazareth—

from a pilgrim writing an amusing account in the sixth century:

We travelled on to the city of Nazareth where many miracles took place. In the synagogue there is kept the book in which the Lord wrote his alphabet, and in this synagogue is the bench on which he sat with other children. Christians can lift the bench and move it about, but the Jews are completely unable to move it, and cannot drag it outside. The house of St Mary is now a basilica, and her clothes are the cause of frequent miracles. The Jewesses of that city are better looking than other Jewesses in the whole country. They declare that is St Mary's gift to them, for they also say that she was a relation of theirs.

Both Byzantine and Crusader churches have occupied the site down the years. The Crusader church was replaced by a church the Franciscans built 200 years ago. Eventually that fell into disrepair and more or less collapsed. The present new basilica was built in the early 1960s by the Italian architect Giovanni Muzio; and Pope Paul VI paid a visit during his Holy Land pilgrimage in 1964, while it was still under construction. The basilica was dedicated in 1968. The courtyard is very striking and worth spending time on; all along the walls are exotic and highly sophisticated mosaics, donated by various countries in celebration of and symbolizing the Annunciation. They reflect the universality of the Church. There are contributions from Thailand, the Ukraine, Slovenia, China ('Our Lady of China, pray for us'), the Dominican Republic, Catalonia, Wales, Glasgow, Malta, Germany, Chile, Colombia and Valencia; one interesting mosaic reads: 'In gratitude from thousands of Polish children, delivered from Russian slavery and Nazi oppression. In the Holy Land and the free world they found home.' There's even one in Esperanto! And there are many more, probably as many as there are countries in the world. Over the main entrance is the complete prayer 'Salve regina' hewn in stone lettering. In the church itself there's a mural towards the high altar donated by the Roman Catholics of Walsingham, the twelfth-century Marian shrine in Norfolk.

In the vast nave of the basilica, under the dome shaped like a lily (a possible meaning of the name Nazareth) Andrew read from his own book of meditations:

Here we are, Lord,
at Nazareth.
Another place that has been in my mind's eye
since childhood.
So this is where you lived
as a child,
as a teenager,
as a young man,
until you left home at thirty.
The hidden years.
I'd like to know more about them, Lord:
there's so much more about you I would like to know.
Perhaps now I shall be able
—still in my mind's eye—to picture
your childhood:
playing in streets so much like these
and working hard in your father's shop.

Also at Nazareth I can begin to understand
why Christians for hundreds of years
have thought your Mother, Mary, to be someone very
special.
Here she was told that she was going to have a son
called Jesus—you, Lord.
Here she was content to be the handmaid of the Lord.
'Let it be to me according to your word.'

Let it be . . .
Let it be, Lord;
whatever is your will for me—
let it be.

Heavenly Father,
  you chose the Virgin Mary
    to be the Mother of the promised Saviour;
We think of her faith and joy, and her devotion to your will;
Give us strength to follow her example;
For the sake of Jesus Christ her Son our Lord.
*(Collects with the New Lectionary)*

### The Church of St Joseph

The present church, built in 1914, is by tradition believed to be on the site where the holy family lived and where Jesus worked alongside Joseph as an apprentice carpenter. A cave in the basement is marked as the actual workshop. Although early Judaeo-Christians came here, believing that to be true, it's hard to find any clear evidence for it. There's an interesting footnote to Nazareth. Charles de Foucauld, the French mystic and recluse, came here in the early part of this century after his conversion from a dissolute life in the army. He wanted to imitate Jesus and live the life he led, among the poor. He worked for a while as a gardener for the Poor Clares in their convent opposite the Galilee Hotel. Some of Charles's clothes are kept there as relics of this holy man. The brothers and sisters of Charles de Foucauld are now spread throughout the world. They follow a very unusual and difficult vocation: they almost invariably choose the most ordinary jobs imaginable—emptying dustbins, cleaning, stacking supermarket shelves and so on—in order to be in touch with those who are obliged to earn their living in this way. I once made a long radio programme about the brothers and sisters, and although I was full of admiration for what they were doing in the world, I must say I still don't fully understand precisely what their vocation is. But that's more my problem than theirs.

### Mount Tabor

After a pretty good lunch in a vast Nazareth pilgrim restaurant which we shared with no one (the owner complaining there were fewer and fewer visitors to the Holy Land these days), we drove about nine or ten miles south to Afula, then turned north-west for the same distance and reached the foothills of Mount Tabor. It's a high peak, some 2,000 feet, and too far to walk up unless you have plenty of time (a good 40-minute hike). There's only one alternative way up—and that's by taxi. Should you go to the Holy Land with any misgivings about the political upheaval, the military presence, the *intifada*, the conflict between Jew and Arab and the international implications of all that, then once you climb into a taxi at the foot of Mount Tabor those considerations pale into insignificance. It's one of the most terrifying and exciting rides I have ever experienced. The drivers are good, they know it, and in their stretched Mercedes-Benz limos they rather care for showing off in front of the foreigners—especially the ladies. We slewed and screeched up and round the tortuous trail in clouds of dust and flying stones. None of us thought we'd make it, but we couldn't pray to prepare to meet our maker for laughing so much. We disgorged ourselves smartly and gratefully at the top, only to realize that the demon drivers would wait for us and take us back down! It didn't bear thinking about.

Mount Tabor is traditionally the scene of the Transfiguration, where Jesus appeared transformed before Peter, James and John, 'up a high mountain'. I think the only way we can begin to appreciate this event is to read the gospel narratives, and try to glean at least some understanding of what took place.

MARK 9:2–8

Six days later, Jesus took with him Peter and James and John and led them up a high mountain on their own by themselves. There in their presence he was transfigured: his clothes became brilliantly white, whiter than any earthly bleacher could make them. Elijah appeared to them with Moses; and they were talking to Jesus. Then Peter spoke to Jesus, 'Rabbi,' he said, 'it is wonderful for us to be here; so let us make three shelters, one for you, one for Moses and one for

Elijah.' He did not know what to say; they were so frightened. And a cloud came covering them in shadow; and from the cloud there came a voice, 'This is my Son, the Beloved. Listen to him.' Then suddenly, when they looked round, they saw no one with them any more but only Jesus.

Throughout the Old Testament particularly, Mount Tabor always had a mystical attraction about it; it's a very dramatic and clean-looking shape rising from the flat plain of Jezreel around it. Neanderthal man came here as long as 80,000 years ago to make his tools; it later proved to be a tactical stronghold where many dramatic battles were fought. It wasn't until the third century that Mount Tabor was considered to be the place of the Transfiguration, and in the sixth century three tabernacles (or small chapels) were built on the summit to commemorate Jesus, Elijah and Moses—as Peter suggested doing in the gospel story.

The other choice for the location of the Transfiguration is Mount Hermon, further north near Caesarea Philippi (Banyas). In many ways Hermon fits better with the gospel accounts. However, like many before us, we settled for Mount Tabor as the place of the Transfiguration.

The Byzantines built here, as did the Crusaders, and there are remains of both eras within the present church, built in 1924 and cared for by the Franciscans. It's a quite beautiful church fashioned in stone which wasn't quarried locally but dragged up the long mountain road on the backs of donkeys. It has two high altars inside: the lower (sunken) one signifying the humanity of Jesus, and the higher (raised) altar showing Jesus' divinity. The summit of the mountain is divided between the Latins and the Greek Orthodox. A wall divides the two churches, which indicates the level of friendly Christian co-operation. Before we went into the church we took advantage of the spectacular views Mount Tabor's height affords of the surrounding countryside and the plain of Jezreel. It was a blustery day and we stood on the ledges and parapets and gazed far out across the plain to distant hills, lost in the hazy sunshine. We could see the Gilboa hills to the south where King Saul elected to fall on his own sword for fear of being captured by the Philistines (1 Samuel), and to the west the plain of Megiddo where Josiah and Ahaziah met their end.

Andrew offered us the opportunity of having a communion service in the church on the summit if it could be arranged. We spotted one of the side chapels to the right of the west door as an appropriate place. This, together with two other chapels, has been built into the present basilica to commemorate Peter's wish that three chapels or booths be built to commemorate Elijah, Moses and Jesus. I volunteered to reconnoitre the land to see if such an 'ecumenical' group, led by an Anglican minister, would be able to avail themselves of the facilities. A rather fierce-looking Franciscan looked horrified at the idea but made signs as though he were going to see what could be done. After some time, and no Franciscan, I pursued him into the sacristy, at which point he gave way and said it would be possible. So, in a side chapel our little pilgrim group had our own communion service. Our pilgrimage to the Holy Land was drawing to a close, and it was good that as Christians from various traditions, we were able to share something like this. As a Roman Catholic, I would have been both angry and mortified if permission had been refused—which it nearly was. After the service, Andrew read from the Old Testament.

Exodus 34:29–35

When Moses came down from Mount Sinai with the two tablets with the Testimony in his hands, as he was coming down the mountain, Moses did not know that the skin of his face was radiant because he had been talking to the Lord God. And when Aaron and all the Israelites saw Moses, the skin on his face was so radiant that they were afraid to go near him. But Moses called to them, and Aaron and all the leaders of the community rejoined him, and Moses talked to them, after which all the Israelites came closer, and he passed on to them all the orders that Yahweh had given to him on Mount Sinai. Once Moses had finished speaking to them, he put a veil over his face. Whenever Moses went into Yahweh's presence to speak with him he took the veil off until he came out. And when he came out, he would tell the Israelites what orders he had been given, and the Israelites would see Moses's face radiant. Then Moses would put the veil back over his face until he went in to speak to him next time.

As we feared, we descended Mount Tabor in our taxis at something approaching the speed of sound, and miraculously came to rest in the car park where our bus was waiting patiently. Some of the group bought souvenirs at the gift shop. Across the road were some Palestinian women with their children, vigorously shaking olive trees and collecting the black olives in sheets they'd placed on the ground underneath. Some squatted and sorted them before putting them into sacks. It struck me that here was a truly biblical scene: local people gathering in the natural harvest on the slopes of Mount Tabor, something which has been going on for many thousands of years.

During the 20-mile journey back to Tiberias, some of us dozed after a fairly exhausting day, and when we arrived at the hotel, we met up with a group who'd been with us on our flight from London. They were on a slightly shorter tour, but were visiting more or less the same locations. After dinner we swapped stories and said it was all too much to take in, all too rushed, and we must all come back again.

**DAY 8**

## The Crusaders and Mount Carmel

The next morning we drove north-west for a good hour to the coast at Acre (Akko), about 14 miles north of Haifa. The name Acre has always been synonymous with the Crusaders to me; and having seen that fine city, I now know why. It was first mentioned in the Egyptian execration texts, 5,000 years ago, when they were listing the places they thought deserving of their curses and general disapproval. Throughout history, Acre has always been independent and the Israelites never really settled here. A little to the south the first Crusaders landed and took the city in 1104; it became the largest Crusader port, far larger than Caesarea, handling merchandise and pilgrims from all parts of mediaeval Europe. In 1191, during the Third Crusade, Richard the Lionheart of England captured Acre from the Muslims who had taken it four years earlier. For the next 100 years it became the capital city of the Latin kingdom controlled by the Crusaders. The famous Templars and Hospitallers set up at Acre. Subsequent Crusades were mounted well into the thirteenth century, and in 1291 these defenders of the holy places against the Infidel were finally defeated and banished from the Holy Land forever. But much of their splendid and robust architecture remains.

If you look on a map you'll see Acre up at the eastern end of the Mediterranean, and therefore strategically placed as a port and a place for approaching and leaving the Holy Land. Marco Polo came here, as did Maimonides, the twelfth-century Jewish rabbi who ended up as physician to the Muslim caliph who besieged the city. St Francis of Assisi passed through on his way to Egypt as a missionary. Those Englishmen who responded to the Crusader call during mediaeval times would have sailed across the Channel to France, marched down to Italy and sailed east on the Mediterranean to Acre port.

We walked down into amazing and vast underground halls, as big as cathedrals, which until recently had been filled with rubble. What a task it must have been to clear the thousands of tons away. We were below the citadel, where under the British Mandate Jewish freedom fighters were imprisoned in 1947. They made good their escape through these Crusader halls. The crypt of St John served as the Crusaders' refectory where hundreds could have sat down together. It's really worth looking at these perfectly preserved remains in detail, and trying to imagine the sort of lives these dedicated men led. Don't miss the walk through the long escape tunnel (almost 200 yards) which Crusaders used to get to the sea when the infidels were storming the ramparts above. We saw platoon on platoon of young Israeli noncommissioned officers, both male and female, on a general education course. This was presumably a history lesson. They all looked about eighteen, which they probably were, and all were armed to the teeth with rifles, machine guns and belts heavy with bullets.

One of the most interesting parts of Acre was the harbour, full of small fishing and pleasure craft nosing into cafés and bars on the seafront. It had a jolly, holiday atmosphere where the temperature was pleasant, the sky blue and the people friendly. We dodged in and out of the old market place filled with fascinating shops and bakeries. Many of these bread shops and patisseries have large circular trays outside on the street filled with nut and honey slices. They are quite delicious and there to be sampled at every opportunity. Time allowed only a whirlwind tour of Acre, but we would all have liked to have lingered a little longer. Its cheerfulness impressed me.

Next stop, Haifa: ten miles or so south along the coast from Acre. This used to be the largest Israeli port before Ashkelon in the south became larger. We stopped at a good vantage point high above this large industrial city and saw the Mount Carmel (Garden of God) range of mountains stretching inland from the coast. The word Carmel is used to denote good wine from the region. This is where the Old Testament prophet Elijah made a sacrifice (1 Kings 18) when he had his contest with the prophets of Baal. It's also the spiritual home of the Carmelite Order, founded in the thirteenth century, which claims kinship with hermits who lived in these mountains. Carmelite priests always include 'our father Elijah' when saying their Masses. At the monastery of Stella Carmel, we were so high, we were almost on the same level as Israeli fighter planes which swooped before us.

Straight down below, near the harbour, is a large building with a golden dome surrounded by the Persian Gardens. It's the world centre of the Baha'i faith, whose founder Baha'u'llah is buried just north of Acre. It's a faith which teaches the unity of all religions and all faiths. Many Baha'i martyrs were created during the 1980s in Iran where they were appallingly treated by Muslim fundamentalists. Andrew mentioned that when he was here some years ago, the QE II luxury liner was at berth filled with American Jews celebrating 25 years of the founding of the state of Israel.

From Haifa we struck south and inland twenty miles to Megiddo in the Jezreel valley, and referred to in the Bible as Armageddon, where the battle of all battles will be fought between good and evil. It's a complicated site (a *tel*) and hides twenty different towns, one built upon another over the centuries. Throughout history this place has been of tremendous strategical importance because, as a fortress, it controlled traffic from north to south of the country through the Carmel range, and following through to the Jezreel valley. When David became king, he decided to fortify certain key cities in his kingdom and Megiddo was one of them. According to the first book of Kings, David's son Solomon turned it into a chariot city. When Solomon took over the fortifications of the towns, his architects had the same design for each of the city gates. When the gate at Megiddo was discovered, the same blueprint was applied to other fortified towns, and the plan was exactly the same, making excavation easier. The *tel* was excavated on a vast scale by the University of Chicago in the

1930s. They spent millions of dollars on the project, the last monumental archaeological project of this type to be undertaken in Israel. The modern style is now more selective, smaller and therefore more economical. There are excellent site-plans to be studied which bring some understanding of double and triple gateways. A very complex *tel* where you need an expert to explain, but worth a visit if only to say you've been to Armageddon!

As the pilgrimage proceeded, I became increasingly interested in the way our group reacted, not only to what we were seeing, but the way relationships developed on a personal and on a general basis. Looking back, I'm sure we were lucky in the sense that we seemed to gel very well. There was genuine interest in where we went and what we saw, and we could all relate the main aspects of our pilgrimage to our religious faith. We had some idea of what to expect, and once that was confirmed, we could then move on to the next location or sequence of events. People's life stories emerged bit by bit; most were untrammelled and ordinary, some were downright eccentric, but others were unexpectedly sad and even tragic. And even in that short space of time, we all became usefully aware of each other's needs, likes and dislikes. We always knew, for instance, who would keep the bus waiting! But no one really minded because it didn't happen to any serious degree. Some were less adventurous than others, but Andrew always gave the option to do something else; the 'catch up with you later' sort of arrangement worked perfectly.

It must be said, however, that Andrew Woodsford, the man who seems to know every nook and cranny of the Holy Land like the back of his hand, was the secret of our success. When there were personal preferences to be satisfied, Andrew knew just what to say to make everybody happy. As a leader he was a mine of information, doling out the facts and the figures in manageable portions. And there was always more—lots more—if you wanted it. Andrew did remark that our group of twelve was the smallest he'd taken to the Holy Land in over twenty years as a leader, which was one of the results of the political upheaval now being experienced in Israel. Perhaps a small, intimate number has an advantage over a large group in terms of time to get to know each other.

One evening, after dinner, I made an arrangement with Andrew for an interview in his room. Like all well-travelled people, he comes well prepared; he had a cup of tea waiting for me made from a clever little container heated by an electrical element plugged into the mains. The temperature was hot and slightly humid, though not unpleasant, and we sat out on the balcony overlooking the smooth and moonlit sea of Galilee. We sipped our tea with powdered milk to the sound of cicadas chirping in the gardens below. Through the clear and unpolluted Galilean air we could see ten times the number of stars in the night sky we'd see at home, crammed in clusters, and winking and sparkling benignly down on our quiet night. It was exciting just being there at that moment, in a region of the Holy Land Jesus had chosen as a special place. He must have known nights exactly like this.

Andrew reminisced about how he'd first come to the Holy Land and his enthusiasm for it. He brought his first group out here in 1969 (eight days for £95!); and he's been back ever since, at least once a year and sometimes more. His enthusiasm is kept alive by two things: every group is different and reactions to the holy places are never the same; and archaeological digs are going on in many sites the whole time, so there's always something new to see, or some new theory to consider. We discussed the number of Palestinian Christians who were leaving the Holy Land for the United States and Europe because of the unsatisfactory political and social conditions in the country. Andrew, and others like him, consider it important to bring as many pilgrims as possible here for their own education, and also to encourage the local Christian communities to hold on. On an almost daily basis there are good reasons shown to us in the media why people should steer clear of this part of the world: we hear of political chaos; we see fighting between Jew and Arab on the streets; and the issue is constantly debated on an international level. The situation seems to get worse as each year passes. How then would Andrew and those like him with their great love of the Holy Land, encourage pilgrims to consider coming on pilgrimage to the Holy Land?

'I think I would begin by expressing to them', he began, 'what one of the early Church Fathers said about the Holy Land. He said it was the "fifth gospel". We are familiar with the written gospels of Matthew, Mark, Luke and John; but to come and spend time here in the Holy Land following in the footsteps of Jesus is rather like having a fifth gospel. To come to the place where Jesus was born, where he exercised his ministry, where he died and where he rose, not in any ultra-pious sense of following his very footsteps, but just to walk down a street and identify with what we know from the gospels; it's a very worthwhile thing to do. We've just been to Mount Tabor for example, which we identify with the story of the Transfiguration, and when we later hear of that event in a gospel reading at church for example, we immediately think of the mountain and view we had of the whole of Galilee from there. That way the story will come alive. The very first time you go to Jerusalem, it's all very confusing. I was very grateful to have spent six months there to get to know all the details, all the back streets, so I can pass that knowledge on to the pilgrims I lead. Some parts are as Jesus would have known them, which to me is something special; and there are other parts, now built over with churches and shrines. And to know that Christians have prayed and worshipped at those places for such a long time has a very moving effect on people. If all the churches in the Holy Land were to become museums—and we've had warnings that this could be the case in the not too distant future—then these sites would not continue to be holy any longer. It's the constant and living worship that keeps them holy, and it would be a great sadness if local Christians were to leave.'

I then mentioned to Andrew my surprise at seeing the humble and very basic type of home Peter, and sometimes Jesus, lived in at Capernaum: those dry-stone-walled shacks between the synagogue and the lakeside. Does this in any way detract from the gospel teaching when we see just how ordinary life was in Jesus' time?

'No, I don't think so. For example: think of someone like St Peter, who, as a fisherman, would have been labelled an unlearned man. And yet when you hear some of the things he said, he shows all the signs of someone with a tremendous insight into human character. The fact that Peter happened to be unlearned was balanced by other companions of Jesus who were learned men. Peter's experience of Jesus gave him such a new understanding of life that he was able to leave the fishing of fish and instead became a fisher of men. We have a hangup that religion has to do with words, whereas Peter and the apostles were far more concerned with deeds and the way in which one behaved. When he spoke of religion it was almost a picture-painting exercise, rather than having long arguments. We have tended to put the words of Jesus, and the apostles, on a pedestal; and that's not where they belong.

'And this, I think, is part and parcel of my fascination with archaeology, because that has to do with the mundane and the everyday: just as religion should be. Theology, faith (whatever you want to call it)—if it's going to mean anything it's got to be something earthy and practical. It was precisely that for the first disciples, and it should be the same for us. Take the basilica they're building over the house of Peter: how much better if they'd left it alone so we could see it in all its simplicity and left it just as it was when it was first excavated. The same has happened in Nazareth: the vast basilica of the Annunciation—beautiful though it is—it's gone way over the top. And the Crusader church it replaced, though it was in a bad state of repair in the early 60s, could have been repaired and would have conveyed a completely different picture. We don't always appreciate that Jesus had a strong sense of humour, and if he had been walking along the shores of the sea of Galilee, he'd have been amused to see what Christians, in his name, have done at the various places in his memory. From a European point of view, you could say the Christian communities in this country have done a disservice to the holy places. The church of the Holy Sepulchre is a case in point. Many Westerners are very disappointed with the way it's presented: shabby, uncared for and a little neglected. But that's the way they do things here and it fits in with local thinking and worship.

'For many people, it comes as a great shock that Jesus was a Jew, and here we are in Israel surrounded by Jews, some of them very observant, some the opposite to that, but most fairly average as far as religion is concerned. Jesus was a reasonably observant Jew of his day; he would have gone to the synagogue every Saturday and gone through all the Jewish rituals and so on, which would be totally foreign to most of us. And unless you have a fair knowledge of that sort of background, I have a feeling you can do a disservice to the message Jesus preached. Although he attracted Zealots, he wasn't one of them; but they thought he was going to be a different type of Messiah than he actually was. It's likely he would have some very strong things to say to the orthodox, religious Jews of today for their fanaticism and extremism. Jesus came from a very middle-of-the-road Jewish family, and they would have kept the major festivals; they would have observed the Sabbath in the home and would have gone to the synagogue. But he wouldn't be the equivalent of the orthodox Jews of today, who are more like the Pharisees in Jesus' time. Those Jews of the strict observance in Jesus' time (the scribes, the Pharisees and some of the rabbis) all disapproved of Jesus—who they realized was growing in importance—because he sat light to the observance of Law, which they took seriously and literally. They reported him to the authorities when he seemed to flout the Sabbath; they tried to catch him out over and over again, and eventually plotted his end successfully.'

I then wanted to know if the nature of the groups had changed over the years. Were they different today from, say, back in the 1960s?

'Because travel is so much easier now, a pilgrimage to the Holy Land is less of a once in a lifetime experience. Many are affluent enough to go to most parts of the world, and a trip here is just one of them. But having said that, I do know some who return time after time because they suddenly realize it means so much more than a trip to the States, or a beach holiday in Hawaii. There are two sorts of groups who come here: those who come from their own church with their own parish priest; but others simply respond to an advertisement somewhere and come alone, ready to meet and mix with a crowd they don't know. This whole idea of having an ecumenical pilgrimage was very much on the mind of Arthur Payton (who founded Inter-Church Travel back in the early 1950s), and his motto was "communication through travel". He felt that if Christians from different denominations came together on a pilgrimage to the Holy Land, or perhaps to Rome, then this would deepen their understanding of each other's faith. The feeling was it would have ecumenical repercussions. And I think this has proved to be true, because nowadays, although there are the very definite Roman Catholic or Baptist pilgrim agencies, most people will join a mixed group and discover that it contributes an awful lot to their understanding of pilgrimage when they get here. Most groups, I might say, do get on remarkably quickly, because they spend so much time together. Often groups grow closer together in adversity, because sometimes the sheer pace of the timetable can become a little punishing.'

# DAY 9

# Caesarea Philippi and the fish beside the lake

**Caesarea Philippi** *(Banyas)*

This was to be our last full day in the Holy Land before returning to England. We made a reasonably early start and headed a little over 40 miles north to Caesarea Philippi. It was fascinating to be driving so close to Lebanon over to the west and Syria to the east. As we approached Caesarea Philippi we could see the hills of Lebanon to the left; barren and deserted now but an area which has seen fierce fighting in the not too distant past. The Greeks were here at Philippi (then called Panyas or Paneas and later corrupted into the Arabic form, Banyas) where they worshipped Pan, the god of nature. Just beyond the car-park there's a red cliff-face carved with niches to accommodate statues of Pan, and some Greek inscriptions are still there. This is one of the main sources of the river Jordan, the river Banyas. A mile to the west of Caesarea is a large wildlife park with a nature trail, where another source of the river Jordan, the river Dan, can be found.

The Emperor Augustus gave this district to Herod the Great, who built a great city here and passed it on to his son Philip who established Banyas as his capital, naming it Caesarea Philippi. After the fall of Jerusalem Titus erected a triumphal arch to commemorate the victory over the Jews, and many prisoners were put to death either by wild animals or being forced to do battle with each other. Little remains of this once great city, which went into steep decline after the Crusaders vacated it in the twelfth century. To date no real excavation has been made of the site, and little is known about what lies underneath the area. In 1967, when the Israelis took it from the Syrians during the Six Day War, it had only 200 inhabitants.

We were now in the foothills of Mount Hermon, the other possible, and perhaps more likely, site of Jesus' Transfiguration. Caesarea Philippi was probably the most northerly point Jesus ever travelled during his ministry. The fourth-century church historian and bishop of Caesarea, Eusebius (260–340), found a tiny bronze statue of the woman healed of the issue of blood (Mark 5:25–34) here. After about an hour looking around and visiting the gift shop (which has information of the wildlife park and the species to be spotted there) we had a reading from Matthew.

MATTHEW 16:13–20

When Jesus came to the region of Caesarea Philippi he put this question to his disciples, 'Who do you say that the Son of Man is?' And they said, 'Some say John the Baptist, some Elijah, and others Jeremiah or one of the prophets.' 'But you,' he said, 'Who do you say I am?' Then Simon Peter spoke up and said, 'You are the Christ, the son of the living God.' Jesus replied, 'Simon son of Jonah, you are a blessed man! Because it was no human agency that revealed this to you but my Father in heaven. So now I say to you: You are Peter and on this rock I will build my community. And the gates of the underworld can never overpower it. I will give you the keys of the kingdom of Heaven; whatever you bind on earth will be bound in heaven; whatever you loose on earth will be loosed in heaven.' Then he gave the disciples strict orders not to say to anyone that he was the Christ.

*A turning point.*
*A watershed.*
*That's what this place is all about.*

*A turning point for Peter.*
*This is where he called you by your name, Lord.*
*'You are the Christ, the Son of the living God.'*
*He wasn't concerned with what other people thought about you.*
*He answered for himself.*

*And he was right.*
*Here at the furthest point you reached in your ministry*
*he got it right.*
*No wonder you said, 'You are Peter,*
*and on this rock I will build my Church.'*

*A turning point for you, too, Lord.*
*From now on you began to talk*
*about going to Jerusalem,*
*suffering,*
*being killed,*
*and rising again on the third day.*
*Did you know about this all along?*
*Or was it something that gradually dawned on you?*
*We don't know.*
*But we would follow your example*
*and follow the hard way,*
*the Father's way,*
*wherever it leads.*

*Almighty God,*
*who inspired your apostle Saint Peter*
*to confess Jesus as Christ*
    *and Son of the Living God:*
*build up your Church upon this rock,*
*that in unity and peace*
*it may proclaim one truth and follow one Lord,*
*your Son our Saviour Jesus Christ,*
*who is alive and reigns*
    *with you and the Holy Spirit,*
*one God, now and for ever.*
                    Series 3 Collect for St Peter the Apostle

Nearby we filled bottles with water at one of the sources of the river Jordan. At this point the water seems to come out of a wall at several places; it then broadens to flow over a shallow weir, then off down the Jordan valley, in and out of the sea of Galilee, and finally into the Dead Sea over 200 miles to the south.

We then travelled south, with Syria over to the east, through the Golan and to Kibbutz En Gev and lunch on the banks of the sea of Galilee. We had a brief tour of the kibbutz and heard a little about how kibbutz members live a life of communal labour and sharing of resources etc. But I somehow felt that the true spirit had now left the kibbutzim; perhaps the kibbutz system has served its pioneering purpose and has had its day.

The real treat in store for us was our fish and chip lunch at the lakeside restaurant, owned by the kibbutz, where we sat down to our St Peter's fish. We were herded into our seats like the first sitting for lunch at a holiday camp! And there overlooking a pool of large fish (not Peter's) we had our tasty fish lunch. Afterwards, for those who wished, a swim in Galilee, and then a leisurely ferryboat across the sea to Tiberias. That was a very memorable trip as we gently made our way across the calm water to the gentle swaying of the boat and into the rays of the setting sun; it prompted all kinds of thoughts about Jesus' public ministry which was largely centred on this inland lake which we were now crossing. To our right, up at the northern tip of the lake, was Capernaum where Jesus spent time with Peter and others drawing parables and analogies from the daily life of a fisherman; and further to the north, the region of Caesarea Philippi, which we had visited that same day, where he moved from village to village preaching and healing. Further south and inland was Nazareth, where Jesus was raised as a child under the care of Joseph and Mary. He'd shown signs even as a child as to who he was; but it was only during the final three years of his life that it became apparent to himself, and those who were willing to follow him, what his real identity and destiny was.

And a good three to four days' walk south, along the hot and dusty tracks and roads, lay Jerusalem: the holy city, David's city and the Temple. It was here, during the last few weeks of his life, when he was a young man of 33, that he knew he had to make the supreme sacrifice.

We spent the evening packing and talking about the journey home the following day.

We had a 5.30 call the following morning and were on the road before dawn by 6.00. It took about three hours to get to the airport, then the usual long wait including a detailed luggage search, passport inspection, and personal questionnaire: Who are you? From where? What have you bought? Who did you talk to? etc., etc. Finally, the duty-free shop which is large, well laid-out and good value for most things. The flight home was uneventful, and, as usual, when we'd landed many of us didn't manage to say our goodbyes in the confusion of the airport. (If you fly El Al be prepared for a long wait at the luggage reclamation; it was a full hour before baggage started to appear at the mouth of our carousel.)

We'd certainly made friends. After all we'd been closely united in our pilgrimage for many hours of every day over a period of nine days. We'd discovered a lot about ourselves, about each other, and about our Christianity. As I said at the beginning, this was my second visit, a visit made richer because it was the second time I had the opportunity of seeing and hearing about those places which must mean so much to any Christian. For this is where Jesus lived; these were the places where he walked and preached and cured the sick. This was the place where he suffered and died for all mankind so that we would be redeemed. I, and all pilgrims who are fortunate enough to visit the Holy Land, have the privilege of walking in his footsteps and learning to know him and understand him more.

If you should ever have the opportunity to go to the Holy Land, whether it be a short pilgrimage or a longer one, take it. Let's remember that in mediaeval times pilgrims from Europe were prepared to walk 3,000 miles and endure six weeks on a less than luxurious, and probably unstable, boat before their pilgrimage proper could begin. Nowadays we're talking of a matter of hours and you're there.

Such a journey will undoubtedly enrich your faith, and you'll be able to say: I was there and I understand just that little bit more about my faith and what it means to me.